SUPERNATURAL
comfort

MARILYN HICKEY

SUPERNATURAL
comfort

trusting God during times of suffering

Marilyn & Sarah
MARILYN HICKEY MINISTRIES

marilynandsarah.org

Supernatural Comfort: Trusting God During Times of Suffering

Copyright © 2025 Marilyn Hickey Ministries

All rights reserved. No part of this book may be reproduced or transmitted in any form or by any means, electronic or mechanical, including photocopying, recording, or by any information storage and retrieval system, without permission in writing from the publisher.

Marilyn Hickey Ministries
PO Box 6598
Englewood, CO 80155-6598
marilynandsarah.org

ISBN: 978-1-938696-49-7

Unless otherwise indicated, Scriptures are taken from the New King James Version®.
Copyright © 1982 by Thomas Nelson. Used by permission. All rights reserved.

Scripture quotations marked NASB are taken from the (NASB®) New American Standard Bible®, Copyright © 1960, 1971, 1977, 1995 by The Lockman Foundation. Used by permission.
All rights reserved. lockman.org

Scripture quotations marked NIV are taken from the Holy Bible, New International Version®, NIV®. Copyright © 1973, 1978, 1984, 2011 by Biblica, Inc.™ Used by permission of Zondervan. All rights reserved worldwide. www.zondervan.com The "NIV" and "New International Version" are trademarks registered in the United States Patent and Trademark Office by Biblica, Inc.™

Edited by Colin McKay Miller.

Assembled and Produced for Marilyn Hickey Ministries by
Breakfast for Seven
breakfastforseven.com

Printed in the United States of America.

CONTENTS

A Note from Marilyn vii

CHAPTER ONE
All Things Beautiful 1

CHAPTER TWO
Corrected Not Crushed 27

CHAPTER THREE
Take Jesus Into Your Pain 47

CHAPTER FOUR
Good Grief 65

CHAPTER FIVE
Power to Overcome Anxiety 85

CHAPTER SIX
The Power of Patience 103

CHAPTER SEVEN

Replacing Strongholds 125

CHAPTER EIGHT

Blessed Thorns 143

CHAPTER NINE

Five Powers for Every Believer 165

End Notes 179
Receive Jesus Christ as Lord and Savior of Your life 183
About Marilyn 185
Learn more about Marilyn & Sarah Ministries 187

A NOTE FROM MARILYN

"No pain, no gain."

Even when I was younger, exercise was challenging. My muscles were so sore that I sometimes found it hard to stand up from stretching or lifting weights.

A fitness instructor will tell you that when you begin to feel pain in your body, that is when you also begin to get the gains. The pain you feel is those muscles being broken down so that new tissue and new muscles can build, and you will be stronger than you were before. Let me say that again: You will be stronger than you were before.

So, is the gain worth the pain? Yes, the gain is worth the pain. Still today I sometimes ask, "I am so sore. Should I be exercising?" Then I think, *Yes, I should, because I am going to gain something good.*

When I was 14, I began memorizing Bible verses. At first it was hard. I could barely memorize one verse, but over time, this spiritual exercise made me stronger. Though I started with one, soon I began memorizing four verses every day! I would say them out loud to everyone I could.

As an adult, I would even pay my kids and grandkids a dollar to memorize verses with me, and every dollar was worth it. Slowly, I saw gains. I memorized 23 books of the Bible. I can no longer recite some like I used to, but when I need the Word, the Holy Spirit brings it back to my heart. You may say, "Marilyn, I could not possibly memorize all that!" It is crucial that we become people of the Word, but spiritual exercise takes many forms. Bible memorization is one of them, but listen, this exercise is not about memorization, it is about transformation! Listen to what God says will happen when you engage in spiritual exercise:

A NOTE FROM MARILYN

Do not be conformed to this world, but be transformed by the renewing of your mind, that you may prove what is that good and acceptable and perfect will of God.
ROMANS 12:2

With spiritual exercise, you stop being shaped by ungodly worldly values, your mind is continually renewed by the Holy Spirit, and others can see God's will through your transformed life. We should all want that! You are never too old to grow closer to God. I am old, so I know what I am talking about.

It is crucial that we become people of the Word, but spiritual exercise takes many forms.

I have learned to gain with God in every season of life. Some of the hardest and highest-gain seasons involved suffering. In those times I memorized 2 Corinthians. It was my daughter, Sarah, who first encouraged me to do so. Second Corinthians is not just a book about how suffering comes, but how to be triumphant in suffering of any kind. Sometimes life was hard, and I needed to know how God would make me triumphant. If stronger muscles can be gained from pain, what can I spiritually gain from the pains of life?

As I learned verses and chapters, I realized this whole book is on sorrow, grief, and pain, but not in a defeated way. It is on how we win over pain and how we can be triumphant in grief and sorrow. In memorizing 2 Corinthians, I saw things I had never seen before. I wish I had learned 2 Corinthians sooner, but sometimes we do not know what we are ready for until God decides it is time.

GOD-POWERED TRANSFORMATION

My late husband, Wally, loved nature shows. Whatever the animal or creature, he watched it. I found the transformation of the caterpillar into a butterfly fascinating because caterpillars are ugly, but butterflies are beautiful. Their metamorphosis brings out many colors. These butterflies may not all look the same, but they were all transformed.

When the New Testament uses the word "transformed," this is the Greek word *metamorphóō*. That's right, a metamorphosis. In his letters to churches, Paul only uses this word twice. Once in Romans 12:2 above and the other time in 2 Corinthians 3:18:

> *But we all, with unveiled face, beholding as in a mirror the glory of the Lord, are being transformed into the same image from glory to glory, just as by the Spirit of the Lord.*

This same word for transformation is used to describe the transfiguration of Jesus in Mark 9:2. In Mark 9, the disciples see the *transformed* Jesus, and they are amazed. This is God-powered transformation! The same Spirit of the Lord the disciples saw in Jesus is at work transforming us, and some of our transformation will only come through suffering. When we look at some of the things that we encounter in life, we do not want to suffer, but we *can* have gains during our trials.

In this book, we will see that God can bring gain out of pain. He brings comfort during our trials and worries. He brings healing. He brings hope. He will bring you through.

*You have turned for me my mourning into dancing; You have put off my sackcloth and clothed me with gladness, to the end that my glory may sing praise to You and not be silent. O L*ord *my God, I will give thanks to You forever.*

PSALM 30:11–12

CHAPTER ONE

ALL THINGS BEAUTIFUL

[God] has made everything beautiful in its time.
ECCLESIASTES 3:11

I find it strange how certain stories stick with us while others do not. Often, the stories we remember are the tales that were passed onto us by our parents, whose parents passed those same tales onto them, and so on. Why, out of all the stories people share, do both young and old know the 1843 Danish fairytale of "The Ugly Duckling" still today? You may not remember all the details, but you know this duckling suffered. It was only after much time and suffering that this duckling realized he was a beautiful swan, one finally strong enough to fly with his new family. Why is it that stories of overcoming suffering resonate so deeply?

Sometimes I think, *How will God bring about good from this painful part of my life?* but then I read Ecclesiastes 3:11 again. He makes *everything* beautiful in its time. This is not often the timing I want, but God likes to get a lot from every experience. Ecclesiastes 3:11 continues, *"He has put eternity in their hearts..."* When I am in a trial, I do not see the big picture of how I could come out of that trial and really be blessed, but God says that the big picture is going to be beautiful in the end. Not ugly like an out-of-place duckling, but beautiful like a swan. Transformed. God is the one who puts eternity into our hearts. This means we can hold on and hold fast that our trials are temporary, but eternity with God is forever. In time, this trial is going to work for your good.

He makes *everything* beautiful in its time.

Thankfully, God does not make us wait until the very end to see His good in our trials.

THE GOD OF *ALL* COMFORT

What are some of the ways God brings beauty during our suffering?

Second Corinthians 1:3 says, *"Blessed be the God and Father of our Lord Jesus Christ, the Father of mercies and God of all comfort."* This is the first thing Paul wants the church in Corinth to know from this letter. Why "all comfort?" Why not just the God of comfort? Because you face all kinds of suffering. Thankfully, God has the right comfort to meet any trial.

You say, "I'm facing financial suffering." Well, God has the right comfort for that. You say, "I'm in a real physical trial and I'm getting bad reports from the doctor." Well, God has the right comfort to go with that physical trial. You say, "I have a relationship problem. They're just so cruel and harsh." Well, God has specific relationship-problem-comfort.

It is key that you see that God is not only that sweet "Father of mercies," but also to remember that God is our strength. The Psalmists knew this. Over 70 times the writers of the Psalms called on God as their strength. Those were people who knew that God's comfort makes you strong.

All suffering will be met by the God of all comfort, and, in time, it will work for your good.

WHERE DOES SUFFERING COME FROM?

We all wonder where suffering comes from. Did God do this to me? Did the devil? Was it my own foolishness? We all wonder, but the answer is not always clear. In John 9:2–3, the disciples asked Jesus, *"Rabbi, who sinned, this man or his parents, that he was born blind?" Jesus answered, "Neither this man nor his parents sinned, but that the works of God should be revealed in him."* Like we often do, the disciples assumed human sin was to blame.

I will be clear: Sometimes sin *is* to blame for the specific suffering. After healing a different man, Jesus warns him, *"See, you have been made well. Sin no more, lest a worse thing come upon you"* (John 5:14). Whether you reap it now or in the future, the wages of sin is death (Romans 6:23). We know that sin can really cause us to suffer. Any Christian can tell you that, because we have all felt the pain after. You might be happy with some of the feelings during the sin, but in the end, the results hurt. It is a reasonable question to ask while suffering, "What is it that I have done?" but our sin is not the only cause.

Job faced tremendous suffering, but it was not due to sin. In Job 1:8, God said to the devil, *"Have you considered my servant Job, there is none like him on the earth, a blameless and an upright man, one who fears God and shuns evil?"*

Suffering can come just from being born in this fallen world. Whether we like it or not, this is a sick world, and sick things happen. We live in circumstances that can bring suffering. Satan is always pressuring you and always wants you to suffer. In the case of Job, we see that Satan was behind the suffering.

In the Bible, there are several words for suffering. Let's look at three of them.

The Narrow Place

I love 2 Corinthians 1:4. It says that it is God *"who comforts us in all our tribulation, that we may be able to comfort those who are in any trouble, with the comfort with which we ourselves are comforted by God."* The word for trouble there, *thlipsis*, means "the narrow place." You know the feeling: It is not just one thing going wrong in your life, but another, then another, and another. Your world gets small. You feel constricted with few options. When you have trouble on all sides, you are in a narrow place. You are moving forward, but you are squeezed through the narrowness of trouble.

Years ago, the evangelist Oral Roberts told me of his mother, Claudius, who had a gift of healing. People would call her when someone was sick. One night she received a call to come to the farm next to them to pray for a young boy who was dying of pneumonia.

> Whether we like it or not, this is a sick world, and sick things happen.

At that time, Claudius was pregnant and in her final trimester. Still, she faithfully ventured out but soon came to a barbed wire fence. Not just a narrow place, but one that could harm both her and her unborn son. She had to stretch up to carefully guide her pregnant belly through. Coming to the boy with pneumonia, she said, "Lord, I don't want this young boy to die. If you will heal him, I will give to you the child that is in me to be a healer to the world." She did not know she was going to have a son. Back then you could not know, but God knew. God knows all the details when we face suffering.

Claudius prayed, God healed, and the boy with pneumonia lived. Claudius soon gave birth to her son, Oral, and he was used by God to bring healing to many around the world.

Would you say her suffering was gain? Would you say that this gain could bless many? How far do you think God might take what you're going through? If you can trust Him and look to Him in your suffering, this is the key.

You may feel pressure and pain from all sides in the narrow place, but God grants armor on both sides. Second Corinthians 6:7 says so: *"By the word of truth, by the power of God, by the armor of righteousness on the right hand and on the left . . ."* You may have pressure on this side and that side, but you have protection in the narrow place. You can believe God will bring you through.

Demonic Attack

For as the sufferings of Christ abound in us, so our consolation also abounds through Christ. Now if we are afflicted, it is for your consolation and salvation, which is effective for enduring the same sufferings which we also suffer. Or if we are comforted, it is for your consolation and salvation.

2 CORINTHIANS 1:5–6

The same root word, *pathema,* used for the sufferings of Christ in verse five is the same word used for the sufferings we endure in verse six. As some of the sufferings Jesus faced were spiritual, some of the sufferings we face are spiritual. A demonic attack can be against your emotions, your body, or your very soul. This type of suffering can occur along with the narrow place of *thlipsis,* but sometimes it is just a demonic attack. You do not feel constricted, but you still do not feel quite right. This spiritual attack can come as a terrible attack on your mental health. It can affect you physically.

You have protection in the narrow place. You can believe God will bring you through.

Oral Roberts told me another story about his mother: Although Claudius Roberts gave him to God to bring healing to many around the world, Oral struggled with tuberculosis as a child. At 17, he nearly died from the disease. He kept spitting up blood and struggled to breathe. What was this attack on his God-given calling? Where was it coming from? Oral went to a healing meeting in a tent. There, an evangelist prayed for him and anointed him with oil. For the first time in his life, Oral could breathe clearly. He quit having blood come out of his mouth, but after years of being sick, his body was weak. As a result, even healed from tuberculosis, Oral struggled to get out of bed. His mother told him, "Oral, I don't feel good about you staying in your pajamas. You're acting like a sick man. You need to get up and get dressed. Then, if you feel tired, lie down in your clothes, but don't stay in your pajamas all day. You're saying to yourself, 'I'm still sick.'" What good advice! Sometimes when we are suffering, all we do is act like there is nothing but our suffering. Sometimes we need to get up, get dressed, and get after the rest of life.

When we hear the stories of faithful people, whether famous or local, we think, *Well, if that person made it through their family struggles, their financial trial, or their health scare, I can make it through, too.* They help us get up and get after life.

Longsuffering

Sometimes you must endure suffering for a long season. There are trials that go on and on and don't seem to get any better. You pray, you believe God, you confess the Word. You get other Christians praying. You seem to be doing everything right, but you do not get better. The trial drags on. This is the third kind of suffering, and I think it is the worst of the three.

The word for "enduring" in 2 Corinthians 1:6 is *hypomonē*, which, when coupled with trials, means longsuffering. It just seems like you keep suffering under the same trial. You wait for it to be made beautiful in its time. You keep on waiting, and then when you are fed up waiting, you have to wait some more. You hold fast to what Galatians 6:9 says, *"Let us not grow weary while doing good, for in due season we shall reap if we do not lose heart."*

> ## Sometimes we need to get up, get dressed, and get after the rest of life.

When I think of longsuffering, I often think of Joni Eareckson Tada. Despite being paralyzed by a diving accident since 17, Joni does not have sad stories to tell you. She has stories of how Jesus is real, wonderful, and mighty. Her suffering may be long, but the comfort of the Holy Spirit goes further. Joni Eareckson Tada knows both the comfort and strength of God, and she shares those teachings with so many through her ministry. The goodness of God in her suffering has become a blessing to many.

Second Corinthians 1:7 says, *"Our hope for you is steadfast, because we know that as you are partakers of the sufferings, so also you will partake of the consolation."* If the suffering is long, if it's *hypomonē*, the consolation is also long. Do not fret about the length of the trial, but rather rejoice in all the consolation coming.

Living in a fallen world, a spiritual attack, or our sin — these are some of the reasons we suffer, yet knowing the source or type of suffering can only help you so much. Do not miss what Jesus said to the disciples about the blind man in John 9:3: That his suffering came about so that *"the works of God should be revealed in him."* This is good news. The work of God always restores good. This helps us remember that the *result* of our suffering matters just as much as the *cause* of our suffering. When you decide to lean into God through this pain, to let him talk to you and deal with you with grace and justice, you get to be one of the first people to see the works of God revealed in your life.

THE PARACLETE

Blessed be the God and Father of our Lord Jesus Christ, the Father of mercies and God of all comfort, who comforts us in all our tribulation, that we may be able to comfort those who are in any trouble, with the comfort with which we ourselves are comforted by God. For as the sufferings of Christ abound in us, so our consolation also abounds through Christ.

2 CORINTHIANS 1:3–5

Life brings new trials, and with it, new opportunities to look to God, to feel His comfort, and to see His good works revealed.

If you look at the word "comforter" in the Scriptures, you will see that *paráklētos* is the basis of the English word paraclete. This is not a common English word today, but paraclete is another word for the Holy Spirit — the one who intercedes, comes alongside, takes your hand, and leads you through. If we will see that God is the God of all comfort, we will expect the Holy Spirit (the Comforter) to guide us through our suffering, but if we do not look for the Holy Spirit during the trial, we can miss Him.

Have you lost your expectation that God will lead you through your trial? Ask the Holy Spirit to guide you and He will bring unique comfort.

LIKE EXERCISE, SUFFERING BUILDS YOUR STRENGTH

Psalm 34:19 says, *"Many are the afflictions of the righteous, but the LORD delivers him out of them all."* God does not say He will deliver us from half of these afflictions, or even most. No, God saves us from *all* afflictions, but we are also told there will be many afflictions for those who follow Jesus. Whether you like it or not, suffering will be a part of your life. Just as exercise builds your physical strength, suffering builds your spiritual strength. Where exercise stretches your muscles, suffering stretches your character.

The *result* of our suffering matters just as much as the *cause* of our suffering.

In suffering we should ask: Is there sin in my life? Is there something God wants to speak to? Is there something He can turn around? Is there something I can learn here? You know you will be stretched by suffering, but you also know God is on the move. It hurts because some of those old ways of thinking and old patterns of living are being broken down. Still, you remember, *I am getting stronger in God through this.*

In your suffering, your pain can become your gain, but it depends on your decision. You must choose to look to the Holy Spirit during your trials.

My son began using drugs as a teenager. It was a really, really hard time. A brutal time of suffering. You can imagine what went through my mind. *I'm the mother, and this is my son involved in drugs.* We could not believe it. I just thought, *It's not true; it's not true.* I tried to deny it until there was no way to deny it. We knew the truth when we found drugs under my son's bed. Then I thought, *I'm the pastor's wife. What are people going to think of us? They're going to think, you can't even raise your kids right. What's going wrong at your house that your kid would get into drugs?*

All this goes through your mind. You are suffering for your child. You are suffering for yourself. You are suffering over what can happen with your friends, your extended family, and your church. But instead of hiding, my husband and I brought it to the church. We believed

God when He said that we should pray when suffering (James 5:13). We believed that *"The prayer of a righteous person is powerful and effective"* (James 5:16 NIV) and we knew we could not do this alone. More than that, we knew that God did not *want* us to go through suffering alone.

You know you will be stretched by suffering, but you also know God is on the move.

This is important: You must bring your suffering to trusted, spiritual members of the body of Christ who will pray for you and stand with you in faith. We told everybody so nobody could gossip. We spoke painful truths from the pulpit. We said, "Our son, Michael, is into drugs, and we are hurting. Would you please pray for us?" Do you know what happened? The church really prayed for us. They spoke the Word over us. They supported and strengthened us. It still hurt, but we remembered the pain was temporary. We remembered that God makes everything beautiful in its time.

We need each other when we are suffering. When hurting, we are tempted to get away from the church, but that is when we need to remain involved, because when we hide, we do not get the consolation only other faithful believers can bring.

Another lesson I learned from watching nature shows with Wally is that wolves never attack the whole herd. They wait for one of the animals to be alone, and then the wolf sneaks in. This loner is usually not strong, but rather a weaker animal struggling to keep up. It may seem easier to fall behind when you are worn out, but you must keep up with your herd.

> **You must bring your suffering to trusted, spiritual members of the body of Christ who will pray for you and stand with you in faith.**

Let me tell you from experience, it is hard for the devil to attack you when you have everybody and their dog praying for you in church. When you withdraw, then Satan says, "I got you. There's nobody supporting you." It is good to regularly meet with those who will hold you up and pray for you, because the wolf does not like to go after a whole herd. The herd is too much of a problem. It is the stray out there that he is going after. It is the one who says, "I'm no longer going to read my Bible. I'm no longer going to pray or go to church. There are too many hypocrites in church." To that I say the church has room for one more. It is better for you to go to church and be a hypocrite than to hang outside of the herd and let the wolf chew you up.

After many years, my son, Michael, learned to live sober. Not only did he have compassion towards those who faced drug addiction, but it did something in me, because I was strengthened to comfort many people whose children face the same trial. I can say to them, "God brought my son through. He'll bring your child through, too." I do not know how much good God brought out of my trial, but I am happy when I reflect on how much is already revealed in helping other people.

COMFORT TO SHARE

If my family had not gone through our trial with Michael, we would not know the specific comfort to give to other parents suffering the same way. Second Corinthians 1:4 makes it clear. We are able to bring this comfort to this specific trouble because we were comforted by God. We often say, "Hurt people hurt people," well, comforted people comfort people! When you receive comfort in the trial and through the trial, that comfort is not just for you, but for others, too. God takes your pain, makes it gain, and stretches it out to bless other people.

Before my long-suffering trial with Michael's drug addiction, I never understood depressed people. I just thought, *Snap out of it. What's wrong with you? Just get up in the morning, read your Bible, and quote 10 Scriptures!* Without meaning to, I lived in my own strength, but then my trial kept going. What used to work no longer worked. I thought, *Wow, I am quoting Scripture and I'm not better.* When I came through that time, I thought, *I'll never knock depressed people again. I'll comfort them. I'll have faith for them the way others had faith for me. I'll have strength for them the way others had strength for me.* Comforted people comfort people.

If I twist my ankle today, the incident will hurt *and* the recovery will hurt, but when I recover well, the gain is worth the pain. You might not have a choice in how you get hurt, but you can choose how you heal.

A twisted ankle is slow to heal, but the body responds with help. Blood flows in and the leg moves differently to support the changes needed. Why would you think it works differently in the church body? Imagine if you cut off your twisted ankle and put it on a shelf, saying,

"I'll just put it away to get well." This is the stupidest thing in the world! You would never do this, because you know your body will help heal the part that suffers. This is why you stay connected to the church through suffering. You need the body to help bring you through, because without the body, you are not going to make it. I do not know how many times people have asked me, "How did you get through that?" and my answer is, "The body helped!"

> **It is better for you to go to church and be a hypocrite than to hang outside of the herd and let the wolf chew you up.**

When you suffer, do not cut yourself off from the church. God made the body to move as one. In 1 Corinthians 12, Paul speaks on how the church body should work together. Verse 18 says that the way God put the church together pleases him, and verse 26 adds, *"If one member suffers, all the members suffer with it; or if one member is honored, all the members rejoice with it."* This is God's design. We rise and fall together. Without the encouragement of fellow believers, we can become hardened in our trial, asking, "Where is God? He allowed this to happen to me. I don't know if the Bible is real, and I don't know if I'm going to serve a God like that." If you do this, you will miss the only true guide who could bring you through your suffering well. You will miss how God uses the church. In suffering, you can get bitter, or you can get better.

God has also placed guides in church. The Bible calls us sheep. Do you know what sheep need? Sheep need a shepherd, but when people pull away and refuse to come under the healthy leadership of pastors and leaders, they can stumble. Why? Because without that guidance and protection, we can go the wrong way. Sheep need shepherds *and* other sheep. Do not turn away from God and His church. You need them too much. As we turn to God, we welcome the Holy Spirit to comfort us. In time, we can comfort others with the comfort and strength received.

YOUR TRIUMPH IS WHERE YOU PUT YOUR TRUST

Now thanks be to God who always leads us in triumph in Christ.
2 CORINTHIANS 2:14

Each day we choose to place our trust in many things: When I sit in a chair, I trust that it will hold me. When I turn the keys in the car, I trust the engine will run. When I turn on a light switch, behold, there is light!

Those are small places of trust, I know, but the principle holds: I trust because of prior experience. When we go through a trial with God, we experience His faithfulness, and in the future, we trust because of that prior experience. In each trial we must choose to trust in God again. We must choose to remember His faithfulness. The most often repeated commandment in the Bible is to remember. Do you know why? Because it is so easy to forget God's faithfulness. It would be strange to marvel at a light switch working every time, but there is no spiritual attack there. Hear me: The devil always wants you to forget or question God's faithfulness. There is spiritual attack on your trust in the Lord. You must choose to remember your trust in Jesus.

God calls us to be triumphant in suffering. Your triumph is where you put your trust. So, what are you putting your trust in? Most importantly, *who* are you putting your trust in? I choose to put my trust in the comfort of the Holy Spirit. He is the God of all comfort. He will not leave me. He is strong enough to take me through.

I put my trust in God, because it says in 2 Corinthians 1:5 that where suffering abounds, comfort abounds. So, you need to get your eyes off your suffering and onto your Comforter.

God will make all things beautiful in your life. He will bring you out better than you ever thought you could be when you went into the trial.

Who knows what God is going to do in your trial? He does! This challenge may be the best opportunity you ever had, so quit looking at the trial and look for the triumph. It sounds simple, but where you look determines what you will see. Hebrews 12:1–2 calls the faithful to focus on Christ:

> *Therefore we also, since we are surrounded by so great a cloud of witnesses, let us lay aside every weight, and the sin which so easily ensnares us, and let us run with endurance the race that is set before us, looking unto Jesus, the author and finisher of our faith, who for the joy that was set before Him endured the cross, despising the shame, and has sat down at the right hand of the throne of God.*

Look unto Jesus. I will say it again, and you say it with me: Look unto Jesus!

Paul was not shy about telling the church the struggles he faced, saying, *"For we do not want you to be ignorant, brethren, of our trouble which came to us in Asia: that we were burdened beyond measure, above strength, so that we despaired even of life"* (2 Corinthians 1:8). Paul faced death. I could understand if he kept his focus there, but look what he says in the next three verses:

> *Yes, we had the sentence of death in ourselves, that we should not trust in ourselves but in God who raises the dead, who delivered us from so great a death, and does deliver us; in whom we trust that He will still deliver us, you also helping together in prayer for us, that thanks may be given by many persons on our behalf for the gift granted to us through many.*
> 2 CORINTHIANS 9–11

Paul credits the church in Corinth for helping by praying for him. Prayer kept him united with the body. He also did not minimize his suffering. The trial was above his strength; he did face death, but what did the trial do? The trial made Paul look to God who raises the dead. Hallelujah! The Bible never says God will not give you more than you can handle. Of course He does! God will never give you more than *He* can handle. He can be trusted to deliver you. Second Corinthians 1:10 says God will keep on delivering us. And who triumphs over death? Jesus triumphs over death: *"Having disarmed the powers and authorities, [Jesus] made a public spectacle of them, triumphing over them by the cross"* (Colossians 2:15 NIV).

> # The most often repeated commandment in the Bible is to remember. Do you know why? Because it is so easy to forget God's faithfulness.

When we speak of suffering, we must speak of the cross. All suffering must be viewed through the mighty, redemptive, and triumphant work of Jesus. We read in Hebrews 12:2 that Jesus endured the cross *"for the joy that was set before Him."* The joy was not *in* the cross, but in what came *from* the cross. Now hear what Jesus says to you:

> "If anyone desires to come after Me, let him deny himself, and take up his cross, and follow Me. For whoever desires to save his life will lose it, but whoever loses his life for My sake will find it."
>
> MATTHEW 16:24–25

Do you desire to follow Jesus? Do you long to find true life? Deny yourself, take up your cross, and follow Jesus. He did not just know of the joy set before Him. He knows of the joy set before you.

GOD USES DEATH TO BRING RESURRECTION

The Holy Spirit always produces resurrection or new life. The rulers in Paul's time sentenced him to death, but Paul knew God had sentenced him to eternal life. He trusted that God could raise him from the dead because he had the lifegiving paraclete of the Holy Spirit — the same power that raised Jesus from the dead, that same power God gifts to you. When we face death, we welcome resurrection power.

I must admit, I do not like Hebrews 5:8 saying that Jesus *"learned obedience by the things which He suffered."* If Jesus learned something, I know I am going to struggle to learn it even more. Bluntly, some of the things we suffer teach us to quit being foolish. We learn to change our thinking, change our talking, and change our behavior. We learn obedience from what we suffer. But Jesus was perfect. His learned obedience caused Him to intentionally limit Himself for our sake, and the agony and weakness He faced on the cross was real.

Still, Jesus said to His heavenly Father, *"nevertheless not My will, but Yours, be done"* (Luke 22:42). In our suffering, we must come to the same place of, "God, just do what you want to do. I surrender to you. I only want your will." If Jesus had not submitted Himself to the Father's will, none of us would see heaven. His pain became our gain. He took our sins and was raised from the dead.

Your pain can be your gain. It just depends on what you do with it. You can choose to seek God's will by asking, "Could this suffering, in time, become beautiful even to me?" You can choose the comfort of the Holy Spirit. You can choose to receive help from your church if you choose to stay connected. In this, there is resurrection power.

CHAPTER TWO

CORRECTED NOT CRUSHED

As we grow older, it is tempting to think our best days are behind us. When it seems like everything is going downhill, you think you cannot look anywhere but down, but I encourage you again to look up to Jesus. Proverbs 4:18 says, *"The path of the just is like the shining sun, that shines ever brighter unto the perfect day."* Are you justified in Christ? Then your path is like a shining sun. Life is not getting darker and darker.

In Christ, life is brightening until the perfect day you stand before God. Even in times of crisis, God gives you an unusual light. Your path gets brighter and brighter.

We must not accept that everything goes downhill as we get older. When we face a trial, we cannot accept the lie that says, "This is normal." I do not believe God calls us to be normal or to simply live in the natural. God calls us to be supernatural. Get out of that "normal thinking" and get into "faith thinking!" Proverbs 4:18 is for us today. We need to live bright.

AN UGLY ISSUE

We have already seen how God can get gain out of pain. We have seen some of the reasons why we suffer and how we can endure suffering, but where can we see God's specific guidance?

In 2 Corinthians 2, Paul revisits an issue that hurt the church in Corinth. Paul is the one who brought correction. This correction was good and right, but it was still painful. Hebrews 12 explains how godly correction works:

> *Endure hardship as discipline; God is treating you as his children. For what children are not disciplined by their father? . . . God disciplines us for our good, in order that we may share in his holiness. No discipline seems pleasant at the time, but painful. Later on, however,*

it produces a harvest of righteousness and peace for those who have been trained by it.
HEBREWS 12:7, 10–11 NIV

The church in Corinth found the discipline Paul brought difficult, but later, what did this discipline produce? *"It produces a harvest of righteousness and peace for those who have been trained by it."* A whole harvest! That is far more than you put in, yet God's discipline is what produces the gain. This is why we do not get discouraged when God disciplines us. Children do need discipline, even if they do not see the benefit at the time. God is so economical! He gets so much out of everything, but if we are not trained by God's discipline, we do not gain this harvest of righteousness. We do not gain its peace.

Get out of that "normal thinking" and get into "faith thinking!"

Just how bad was this church in Corinth? Before Christ, they were heathens living in gross sin. As a naval port, Corinth could import and export sin easily. When these sailors landed, it was party time. It was drunkenness and immoral sex and anything they wanted to do, and what they wanted to do was everything God told people not to do. It was an ugly scene in Corinth, probably one of the most immoral cities of the day.

Paul planted this church, but the people who got saved in this immoral city came with immoral backgrounds. Paul longed to see his new converts experience the abundant life of Christ, but their ongoing sin was only going to steal, kill, and destroy what God had planned (John 10:10). The problem for Corinth was that, even in church, even after coming to Christ, they still lived in gross sin.

"How bad could it be?" you ask. Oh my, it was bad. I cover my eyes as I write this. In his previous letter, Paul tells us that it was *"such sexual immorality as is not even named among the Gentiles — that a man has his father's wife!"* (1 Corinthians 5:1). There are sins so great that we do not even want to name them — apparently even the secular world of Paul's day did not want to speak of this — but here a man in the church was involved in sexual sin with his stepmother. Yuck, yuck, yuck! Suddenly, discipline for this man makes sense. When you see how damaging sin is, you see how necessary God's discipline is. The sooner you see the need for God's discipline in your own life, the better.

You may be thinking: *Marilyn, why are you sharing all this ugliness? I know it's in the Bible, but help me see the good.* Remember, 2 Corinthians is all about how to triumph through pain and suffering. It is a beautiful book about how to honor God in ugly times. We must speak of ugliness to see how beautiful Jesus can be to us in it. Every one of us has pain in our lives, but pain can be productive or destructive. Pain can make us give up or pain can make us look up to Christ. Which shall we choose?

The sooner you see the need for God's discipline in your own life, the better.

What did Paul do with this mess in Corinth? He disciplined the church and instructed them to *"put away from yourselves the evil person"* (1 Corinthians 5:13). This sexually immoral man was so destructive that they had to kick him out of the church in the hopes that he would repent. This decision is not made lightly, but if someone keeps willfully sinning, you need to put this person out of the church because sin is contagious.

If you don't deal with that spreading infection in the body, then soon somebody else is going to say, "Well, if he can live like that, what I'm doing is okay." It is the grace of God that keeps sin from continually spreading throughout the church. This is a heavy warning: If you do not cut sin out of your life, you run the risk of being cut off from believers who are walking in righteousness.

If you did not know the source of the incident, the behavior of the man in the church of Corinth might sound like a recent story because there is so much sexual sin in society today. Not just around the world, but in the church. We cannot just close our eyes and say, "It's not there." We are going to have to cause some pain in order to produce more life.

RESTORATION FROM CORRECTION

O Lord, correct me, but with justice; not in Your anger, lest You bring me to nothing.
JEREMIAH 10:24

You may think, *Where is the triumph in a man sinning so wildly that he got kicked out of the church of Corinth?* But like I said in my autobiography, when it comes to the move of God on your life, it is not over until you win. Second Corinthians continues the story. In 1:23–2:4, we learn that the pain caused by Paul's correction was so great that he did not go back to Corinth, but instead sent this loving letter.

Pain can be productive or destructive. Pain can make us give up or pain can make us look up to Christ.

We learn in chapter 8 that this letter came with Titus. My husband, Wally, and I learned a similar lesson as pastors: Sometimes when you correct someone and it hurts, others may need to be brought in to make sure the graceful intent remains. That person may go to different people or a different church, but they will not escape God. If God wants to correct, it may hurt, but that pain leads to repentance and produces life. When you are corrected, this view helps you say, "This is good for me."

Paul's love for the church in Corinth drove his correction. It even hurt him to do so, but Paul knew the threat of sin. Well, time went by between these two letters. God was on the move. Did the man caught in sexual sin repent? Was he restored to the church? Though unnamed — and, boy, if this was your sin, you would be glad you went unnamed in the Bible — many believe 2 Corinthians refers to that same man. Paul writes:

> *This punishment which was inflicted by the majority is sufficient for such a man, so that, on the contrary, you ought rather to forgive and comfort him, lest perhaps such a one be swallowed up with too much sorrow. Therefore I urge you to reaffirm your love to him.*
> 2 CORINTHIANS 2:6–8

Hear me: The correction of removing the man from the church was to save him, not to crush him. When we bring correction, we also bring forgiveness and comfort, and we reaffirm our love, even if we have to hold the line.

Sexual immorality is still wrong. Watching pornography, sleeping with someone who is not your spouse, and all kinds of sexual perversion that may take on a new form tomorrow — all of it is still wrong. It does not matter how many in our culture accept the sin; the church must not look the other way. Otherwise, your church will be ensnared in the same sin. This is nothing to shrug your shoulders at because sin produces death. How many of us want death? I do not. I want life. How about you?

Maybe you have someone on your heart as you read this and you say, "Marilyn, they're in such awful sexual sin." Pray for them! Do not just shake your head and say, "It's impossible. They won't change." Look to Jesus. He says, *"With God all things are possible"* (Matthew 19:26). God can change anyone. He can transform anyone. The man involved in sexual sin was transformed when everybody in the church got on the same page. It was not just a few faithful voices who said it was wrong.

The correction *"was inflicted by the majority."* A church united under God's will is a powerful force. As the church, we need to stand on the same page and be clear about what is right and what is wrong. Sometimes it hurts, but in the end, correction produces life. After all, we are correcting people's paths back to Jesus. *"The wages of sin is death"* indeed, *"but the gift of God is eternal life in Christ Jesus our Lord"* (Romans 6:23).

Stand up for what God says. Stand up for your home. Stand up for your church. Stand up for your community. Stand upon the Word and its promises. Do not fear worldly criticism or consequences. If it hurts these places to put the squeeze on, if it hurts you, then let it hurt, because Godly pain produces repentance, and repentance produces salvation.

That's what Paul says later in 2 Corinthians 7. He does not regret that his letter brought pain because that pain brought about what God was after, *"For godly sorrow produces repentance leading to salvation, not to be regretted; but the sorrow of the world produces death"* (2 Corinthians 7:10). You will never get gain out of pain that was caused by something from which you have not repented. You will never get the gain without turning back to God. God uses pain. That is why it comes into our lives. So, do you want the benefit of pain or are you going to waste it? Even worse, are you going to let the enemy use pain to produce death in you?

Paul wrote about how we come out of correction. The conviction of sin is good, but the devil can even work there. The corrected man could be *"swallowed up with too much sorrow"* if everyone kept piling on, repeating, "Remember what you did! You caused a lot of trouble with this church." Sometimes, it is easier to be obedient in tough love than in extending comfort and forgiveness, but without those, the corrected person can become so depressed and disappointed that they never see God's redemptive hand at work.

Without the redemptive ministry of Jesus, Satan sinks people with worldly sorrow. We are not trying to crush people and destroy them. We are in this to save them. We want their pain to be gain, not to bring destruction. How would this be God's correction if the man did not experience Christ's forgiveness over his sin? How would this be God's correction if the man never returned to church? How would this be God's correction if the man felt so condemned that he sinned all the more and even took his own life? Forgiving means you move on. You bring comfort and reaffirm your love. Paul *urges* this. The cross demands it.

We need to have the same approach with our children. They often receive our correction, but do they receive our forgiveness, comfort, and continued affirmations of our love? When I first went away from home to university, I pursued the wrong things. Soon, I felt so bad about it. I told my mother and she did not condemn me. She did not scream, "How dare you! How could you do those stupid things after all I've taught you?" She instead said, "I'm glad you're sorry. I'm so glad you felt you could come to me, Marilyn, and God forgives you if you've repented."

I continued, "I'm still so sorry! I feel so unclean."

She said, "Take the cleansing of Jesus, take the forgiveness of Jesus," and she comforted me. She gave me hope that I still had a good future.

I will say to you parents, be careful. Yes, correct your children, but do not crush your children. You may know better than they do, but you do not know better than God. There is a difference between correction and crushing. Maybe you know what it is like to be crushed, saying, "I've been so corrected and so crushed in it. It still hurts." To that I say, let the pain of your correction become your gain. Let God love you, bring you through, and make you victorious.

PEOPLE CAN BE YOUR TEST

For to this end I also wrote, that I might put you to the test, whether you are obedient in all things. Now whom you forgive anything, I also forgive. For if indeed I have forgiven anything, I have forgiven that one for your sakes in the presence of Christ, lest Satan should take advantage of us; for we are not ignorant of his devices.

2 CORINTHIANS 2:9–11

This is not the first test Paul gave to the church in Corinth. It would not be the last. After all, he wanted them to be *"obedient in all things."* People can be our test. Are we going to pass this test the way the Bible teaches? Are we going to miss it or even blow it? Are we going to crush people with bitterness and unforgiveness? Will we withhold comfort and no longer speak out our love? It is a test for them, but it is a test for us, too. Will we handle this test in the wisdom of God? I keep praying, "Lord, help me to pass the test when I have to correct people. Keep my motives pure and focused on saving them. Let this be truly redemptive." Isaiah 53:5 says, *"By his wounds we are healed"* (NIV). There are wounds, yes, but in God, there is also healing. My motive is to pass the test with God.

You will never get gain out of pain that was caused by something from which you have not repented.

We do not compromise in confronting, but we do not compromise in restoring either. Sometimes you really want to go after people, saying, "You idiot, how could you get into this sexual lifestyle that hurts your spouse, hurts your children, hurts everything? How could you not think of them?" But we cannot crush them because we are in a test, too. Instead, we pray for God to give us the grace to confront not compromise, to lovingly correct and to not crush.

If we can save people, help pull them out of that lifestyle, we can save them from the burning fire of what the devil was using to absolutely destroy them. Paul wrote that he is joining the church in forgiveness, doing so for their sake. He tells them how to forgive.

Forgiving means you move on. You bring comfort and reaffirm your love.

I will never forget the following Scripture as long as I live. He says we forgive *"in the presence of Christ"* (2 Corinthians 2:10). You are more careful when you know the teacher is watching. The King James version says we forgive *"in the person of Christ."* There are many things I cannot do in Marilyn Hickey, but I can do them in Jesus Christ. Jesus gives the grace to do what is necessary. Forgive in the person of Jesus Christ.

I love this section! It is so wonderful. Even the warning contains a blessing. We forgive, *"lest Satan should take advantage of us; for we are not ignorant of his devices"* (v. 11). You have actually learned from your previous tests! You are not ignorant of the devil's devices. You know Satan does not want you to obey God. When you do not forgive, when you withhold comfort, when you do not reaffirm your love, Satan takes advantage of that person and could destroy them, but he also takes advantage of you and puts bitterness in your heart. Bitterness can never make you better. It can only make you worse.

In getting older, I have seen how decisions, good or bad, affect the generations to come. It is not just that we alone get bitter or better. Our choices impact our families. I know a family where the father got involved in heroin. Bad news. He deserted his family, left his wife alone to raise their three girls and a boy in the Lord, but the son got hooked on heroin just like the father. This son was not even around the father, but he had never supported them, which made the boy bitter. Finally, the son met the father and beat him up. He was so angry at how the father's choices hurt him. But then, what he hated in his father, he began to do. His life was steered by heroin. He, too, fathered a child he deserted. Yet if someone brought up how he was acting, he did not see what was wrong because he was still full of bitterness towards his father.

The judgments we use come back on us. They open us up to live similarly. That is an advantage Satan can get if you let him. If you do not forgive, you could end up living the same way. You may be able to say, "Well, I never slept with my mother-in-law or my father-in-law. I never did heroin or abandoned my family." Do not brag about what you would not do. You do not know what you would do if Satan came at you outside of the presence of Jesus and the grace of God.

The biggest way Satan can get an advantage is through unforgiveness. Peter once asked Jesus how many times he needed to forgive the same person. We have all read about the disciple Peter in the Gospels. Whatever he thought, he said. Whatever happened in his life, he blurted it out. This means Peter likely asked this forgiveness question about a real person causing him real hurt. He wanted to know, "How long until I don't have to deal with this person anymore?" Instead, Jesus told Peter a parable about an unforgiving servant. This servant could not pay his debt, but the master mercifully forgave it anyway. Yet this same servant went out and refused to forgive the debt of another. So, how does Jesus answer Peter's desire to withhold forgiveness? How does the parable end?

> *"Then his master, after he had called him, said to him, 'You wicked servant! I forgave you all that debt because you begged me. Should you not also have had compassion on your fellow servant, just as I had pity on you?' And his master was angry, and delivered him to the torturers until he should pay all that was due to him.*
>
> *"So My heavenly Father also will do to you if each of you, from his heart, does not forgive his brother his trespasses."*
> MATTHEW 18:32–35

The way we forgive should reflect how much Jesus forgave us. The young man who was bitter at his father is still on my heart, and I pray that he will forgive his father. Until he does, he will likely continue to struggle with heroin and will continue to fail his family. That is what his father did. That is what he now does. The patterns he despises in his father are now his own. Sin produces death, a cost too high for you to pay, but when we repent, godly sorrow produces repentance that leads to salvation. It produces life. Jesus can set you free to walk in what will become gain.

I began this chapter with the truth of Proverbs 4:18: *"The path of the just is like the shining sun, that shines ever brighter unto the perfect day."* We can live brightly through correction — ours or others. Second Corinthians 4:6 tells us how our lives should look: *"For it is the God who commanded light to shine out of darkness, who has shone in our hearts to give the light of the knowledge of the glory of God in the face of Jesus Christ."* I hope you have met a believer with a radiant heart for God. They brighten the room. They lift your eyes in a dark trial to the sun breaking at dawn.

But 2 Corinthians 4:3–4 also brings a warning as to the dampening power of sin: *"Even if our gospel is veiled, it is veiled to those who are perishing, whose minds the god of this age has blinded, who do not believe, lest the light of the gospel of the glory of Christ, who is the image of God, should shine on them."*

Sin and unforgiveness blind us to the shining glory of Christ. This is the work of the devil, and you, dear believer, know better than to fall into this scheme. Live bright.

The path of the just is like the shining sun, that shines ever brighter unto the perfect day.

PROVERBS 4:18

For it is the God who commanded light to shine out of darkness, who has shone in our hearts to give the light of the knowledge of the glory of God in the face of Jesus Christ.

2 CORINTHIANS 4:6

CHAPTER THREE

TAKE JESUS INTO YOUR PAIN

I am thankful that God knows what He is doing through me even when I do not. People will tell me things I have said that truly helped them. Some I remember, many I do not. In all cases, if those words drew people to Jesus, it was the Holy Spirit speaking. When a situation is heated, I know I need the Holy Spirit to speak then, and thankfully, He does. Jesus told His disciples:

> *"When you are brought before synagogues, rulers and authorities, do not worry about how you will defend*

yourselves or what you will say, for the Holy Spirit will teach you at that time what you should say."
LUKE 12:11–12 NIV

The Holy Spirit can still guide how we speak today. You may not face conflict before your church or local authorities over your faith, but conflict will come your way. We have all looked back and thought, *I should have said this* or *If only I knew the right Bible verse to say,* but more is needed than the right words. There is so much going on in any conflict that what we know or observe will not be enough to reach what God is after. Thankfully, the Holy Spirit teaches us what to say at that time. He puts that miracle in your mouth. We cannot even prepare for this in advance, but we can trust God's guidance.

The Holy Spirit guiding our speech does not mean that we will always get the result we want. Look at Jesus. He always spoke truth and wisdom. Doing so made people want to stone Him, throw Him off a cliff, and crucify Him. But we can trust that the work of the Holy Spirit will bring about the will of God. This Comforter, this paraclete of the Holy Spirit, will teach us to speak when people come against our faith. This truth strips the worry from that future.

Remembering the faithfulness of God in the past and hoping in the teaching of the Holy Spirit in the future — both help us to trust Jesus in the present. Nowhere is this more clearly emphasized in your life than in times of pain. Yes, it hurts, but you also know God is with you.

IT'S ALL ABOUT THE PRESENCE OF CHRIST

I was a pastor's wife for decades. I loved that time serving with my husband, Wally, under the guidance of the Holy Spirit. Looking back, I think being a pastor's wife was one of the highest honors I ever had. That role taught me to really practice what I preach because the people in the church knew me. My strengths shone through to them, but so did my weaknesses. All their strengths and weaknesses became clear, too. Together, we learned to trust God for His Spirit and His Word to bring us all through.

Just like with Paul in his church in Corinth, Wally and I had to correct people in our church. We found that often, even when you correct people lovingly, they run. They get offended, ignore the issue, and never get cleaned up. Again, you will never get gain out of pain that was caused by an unconfessed sin. You will never get the gain without turning back to God.

I once corrected a woman because of how she treated her children. She would scream at them and say the most horrible things. She was a born-again believer, but she was always negative and always putting her children down. I said, "You are speaking death into your children's lives when you have promises of life to speak over them. That's what they need to hear from you." She got so angry with me, saying, "Who are you to tell me what to do? You're not perfect. I've seen how you are." She left the church, and her children did not turn out well. To this day, as far as I know, she does not attend church anywhere.

> Together, we learned to trust God for His Spirit and His Word to bring us all through.

Some say, "Don't correct people like that. You'll just run them out of the church," but we cannot compromise God's Word. Pain has gain in it, but if we choose incorrectly, it will instead produce death. This woman had pain, but she did not let it become gain because she did not take it into the presence of Jesus. I have already told you about some of the pain with my children. This woman was right: I am not perfect, but we take our pain to the one who is.

Hebrews 4:15–16 reminds us that *"we do not have a High Priest who cannot sympathize with our weaknesses, but was in all points tempted as we are, yet without sin. Let us therefore come boldly to the throne of grace, that we may obtain mercy and find grace to help in time of need."*

There are many places pain can take you, but you must bring it all back to the same place: the perfect presence of Jesus Christ.

THE WINNING FRAGRANCE

Walk in love, as Christ also has loved us and given Himself for us, an offering and a sacrifice to God for a sweet-smelling aroma.
EPHESIANS 5:2

In 2 Corinthians, after encouraging the church to forgive the man who was previously caught up in sexual sin, Paul tells of his travels. He saw God opening doors for him, yet still had no sense of rest in his spirit, because he felt he needed his brother in Christ, Titus. We may be tempted to say, "My goodness, Paul, are you that dependent on Titus?" but evidently, he was. After all, none of us — not even Paul — can do the ministry God has for us alone. We learn to respond to unrest in our spirits, so Paul set out to find Titus. Upon finding him, Paul remarked, *"Now thanks be to God who always leads us in triumph in Christ, and through us diffuses the fragrance of His knowledge in every place"* (2 Corinthians 2:14).

This is one of my favorite verses. God says, "I always want you to win." Well, in my natural thinking, I do not think we are always supposed to win. Yet in my supernatural thinking, I learn that if we live life the Bible's way, we do always win. Second Corinthians 2:14 does not say we will win half the time or even most of the time. It says God *always* leads us to triumph in Christ. This is God-led victory. You need to memorize this Scripture. You need to know where your triumph lies. Where? In Christ, not without Him. Put your hand on your heart. Say, "I won't forget. I always win in Christ, not without Him."

In triumph, Christ diffuses the fragrance of God's knowledge everywhere. When we win, it gives off a winning fragrance better than any cologne or perfume.

When we win, others say, "It smells like winning. If they can win, so can I." There is nothing else like it!

We often think of how our lives would change if we lost our vision or hearing, but God gave us five senses to navigate this life. Experts believe our sense of smell has deep connections to old memories and current emotions. Some therapists believe that odors can be used to help us heal. No wonder people buy cologne, perfume, and scented candles. For me, the smell of popcorn is tied to many fun family memories. Other scents remind me of specific people, and yes, some odors remind me of painful times in my life.

> **I won't forget. I always win in Christ, not without Him.**

Maybe you say, "There's no fragrance on me called winning. It's just the opposite. It's losing. It's a bad odor." But I believe God has a winning situation for you. I believe it is in His Word. It is in repentance. It is accepting that what God says is more than what you think, more than your hurt, or more than your depression. If you are willing to be honest about yourself and what is going on, this teaching will cause you to triumph in Christ. Not part of the time, but all of the time. In the natural, we can look and see places where we won, but we also see places where we lost. Yet in Christ, all of this is gain.

I think about the night I truly committed to being a born-again Christian. Although I was in church and had interest in God in the years prior, I did not know repentance until this night. I was 16, pained by my past and my sin coming up before me, but when I repented, it was gain to receive Jesus and to get saved. I have never forgotten that pain, and I have never forgotten how God used it to steer my life for good. That one prayer that night changed my life. God is still working through that prayer all these years later. That pain brought repentance, and that repentance brought salvation. Do you think I am sorry that my name is in the book of life? Do you think I am sorry that I am going to heaven and not to hell? No! One prayer can change your life forever and give you eternal life. You have a divine appointment with God.

Maybe you say, "Marilyn, I prayed a similar prayer, but my lifestyle is still not good." Our sins may be different, but our way back to God is the same. Repentance leads to salvation, and salvation is deliverance. In fact, one of the meanings of salvation *is* deliverance. If you are not where you should be with God, with all my heart I challenge you to pray and recommit your life to Christ. He can refresh you and renew you and turn your situation around.

There are times where life will squeeze out what is inside of us. As long as things do not get too stressful, we can pretend we have it all together, but when we are truly pressed, the truth of who we are comes out. If you are angry or a worrier, that will come out. If you are hopeful or have learned the peace of God in all circumstances, that will come out.

Repentance leads to salvation, and salvation is deliverance.

This is God's grace! If we never face hard times, we will not know who we truly are. God allows hardship to press out the reality of our faith in Him. In the same way that perfume is released when the spray nozzle is pressed, the fragrance of the knowledge of God often comes out when we are pressed. Whatever the season, no matter the pain, this triumph is the winning fragrance.

TWO THIEVES, TWO RESPONSES

For He made Him who knew no sin to be sin for us, that we might become the righteousness of God in Him.
2 CORINTHIANS 5:21

Pain brings a choice into our lives. Will we take Jesus into our pain? Will we let Him talk to us and cleanse us and transform us by the pain, or will we just get bitter and never get better?

> If we never face hard times, we will not know who we truly are.

I believe one of the best examples of this is the two thieves on the cross (Luke 23:32–43). When Jesus was crucified, He was placed between these two thieves. Both were guilty. Both were crucified on their crosses. They both suffered immense pain and both wanted to come down. When we are in pain, often all we can think about is getting away, but getting out of the pain will not bring the gain God desires. I wonder if those thieves would have changed without facing the pain. Probably not. They would have gone back to stealing again. The cross was there to change them. The pain was there to transform them. Time grew short for both, but one made the choice to turn to Jesus, the other did not.

The first thief said, *"If You are the Christ, save Yourself and us"* (Luke 23:39). He thought that if Jesus was the Messiah, He should not be dying on a cross, and he mocked what he did not understand. But the other thief replied:

> *"Do you not even fear God, seeing you are under the same condemnation? And we indeed justly, for we receive the due reward of our deeds; but this Man has done nothing wrong."*
>
> *Then he said to Jesus, "Lord, remember me when You come into Your kingdom."*
>
> *And Jesus said to him, "Assuredly, I say to you, today you will be with Me in Paradise."*
> LUKE 23:40–43

The second thief saw the ugly truth about himself, but he also saw the beautiful truth about Jesus. He was transformed — not by coming down from his cross, but by accepting his cross. Like the thief, your time of following Jesus may be short, or it may be long, but if you desire to follow Jesus, His command to you is the same: Deny yourself, take up your cross, and follow Him (Matthew 16:24).

How can you accept your pain unless you take Jesus into it? The thief was transformed in his pain because he saw Jesus as his savior. He saw Jesus' kingdom. The people on the ground did not see it. The priest did not see it. The other thief certainly did not see Jesus' kingdom. It was the thief who embraced his cross and saw the Messiah on His cross. He was the one who ended up transformed and went to heaven. The other thief stayed the same and went to hell. He endured the same pain but got no gain. The pain brought him destruction, not life. What was the difference? One sinner looked to Jesus from his cross, the other did not. Which one are you?

What will bring transformation to your pain? Seeing Jesus in your pain.

Two thieves faced the same situation, yet only one turned to Jesus. Even Paul recognized the winning fragrance of Jesus is not received the same way by people: *"For we are to God the fragrance of Christ among those who are being saved and among those who are perishing. To the one we are the aroma of death leading to death, and to the other the aroma of life leading to life"* (2 Corinthians 2:15–16).

NOTHING WORSE THAN WASTED PAIN

I constantly remind myself that *"as the sufferings of Christ abound in us, so our consolation also abounds through Christ"* (2 Corinthians 1:5).

There are times so crushing that all we can do is *let* Jesus into our pain, but often, in longer trials, we must willingly *take* Jesus into our pain. The choice to journey with Jesus even in the hardest trials is what brings transformation. If we take Jesus into our pain, Jesus can give us His consolation, but without Him, we do not have that comfort. We cannot be like the thief on the cross who refused to believe in Jesus but still wanted the benefits, saying, *"If* you are God, you will save me."

If we do not welcome Jesus to deal with us and show us how to be honest with ourselves, even in pain, there is no transformation for us. You may say, "I can't believe the pain of losing a loved one could become my *good* transformation." You may say, "I don't see how all the hurt done to me would be something God can use." We can all throw our hurts before God and question what we think He should have done, but our reality is better. It is not getting darker and darker, but one that is getting brighter and brighter in Jesus Christ.

So, will you let Jesus in and trust that He will do a good work in your situation? You may be tempted to say God is to blame. We should blame God for the *good* in our lives, not the bad. We should ask Him, "Where am I to blame? Is there anything in me you would like to talk about?" King David knew that there was nowhere he could escape from God's presence (Psalm 139:7), and he invited God to examine him:

Search me, O God, and know my heart;
  Try me, and know my anxieties;

And see if there is any wicked way in me,
  And lead me in the way everlasting.
PSALM 139:23–24

Get God into your pain. He brings transformation, and this transformation is your gain. I think there is nothing worse than wasted pain — to suffer anyway but to miss what God is after. God always wants us to gain from our pain, and we cannot distance ourselves from him without distancing ourselves from the comfort and transformation He wants to bring.

The choice to journey with Jesus even in the hardest trials is what brings transformation.

All suffering can have a reason and a purpose if we bring Jesus into it. I have a dear friend whose husband began engaging with another woman. He would call, send letters, and even send money to the other woman. I do not think he was sexually involved with her, but it was heading in that direction. This was devastating to my friend. Twenty years of marriage looked to be crumbling. She was a good wife, a good mother to their children, and this is how he behaved. At times she was angry, at times she was sad. She did not know what to do, but we prayed that Jesus would show Himself to her in this trial. She did this because her husband did not think that she knew of the other woman. My friend knew she only had one chance to get this conversation right. I could only support her so much, but God was always with her. She let Jesus into her pain, and in her time of conflict, the Holy Spirit taught her what to say.

My friend told her husband, "I know what you are doing. I've seen the letters you wrote on the computer. I saw where the checks went," but then she asked, "What is it I could do to help you or show my love to you?" This is not normal thinking; this is Word thinking, but I tell you, her husband broke down and wept. He told her that he previously had a child out of wedlock before he married her. He wanted to get in touch with the child to see if he could help. So, he wrote letters and sent money through the mother of this child. He said, "I never thought I could come to you. I thought you would be angry. I thought you might leave me."

> There is nothing worse than wasted pain — to suffer anyway but to miss what God is after.

I can see all the ways that this painful trial was unfair to my close friend, but what I remember is her gain. She forgave her husband, and their marriage is strong still today. She got in touch with the other woman and led both her and the child born out of wedlock to Christ. My friend's pain became gain when she brought Jesus into the situation. The transformation was not just for her, but for others. If instead, everything fell apart, I would have understood. I would have said, "That's just normal," but God wanted better, and my friend chose to see what God could do in her pain. Romans 2:4 reminds us that it is the kindness of God that brings us to repentance. Why should we be surprised when God calls us to extend that same kindness when we are wronged?

All suffering can have a reason and a purpose if we bring Jesus into it.

My friend triumphed in Christ. Through her pain, God diffused the fragrance of His knowledge to her husband, to the other woman and her child, and to all those who have heard this story over the years. The winning fragrance of Christ is wonderful among those who are being saved, but among those sinning, it causes them to feel condemned. Not everyone will respond the same way, but some will see life.

One thief embraced his cross because he saw Jesus; the other hated his cross and could not see Christ. The very fragrance of victory for one thief became the fragrance of destruction for the other. We come back to the choice. Do I choose to be transformed in my pain?

Do I choose to bring Jesus in? One way is going to bring salvation and deliverance, while the other will bring death. You choose. You cannot blame anybody else.

You can have Jesus Christ and His presence in your circumstances. The Holy Spirit can teach you in your times of conflict. With God, you can come out winning. When we embrace our cross, Jesus can speak to us because our hearts are open. If God has not spoken into your situation, maybe you do not want Him to say what He needs to say. Jesus always brings new and abundant life. He can create a new beginning for you, even if it does not look like what you expected.

We always win in Christ, never without him. Which do you choose?

CHAPTER FOUR

GOOD GRIEF

Growing up, people used to say, "Good grief!" when confronted by something unbelievable. These days, the only time I hear that phrase is on Charlie Brown TV specials, but it got me thinking: Is there such a thing as good grief? We assume all grief is bad, but as explored in the previous chapter, when we study the Scriptures, we see that God can work all things for our good. Still, what about our greatest times of loss? What about when we mourn?

Sometimes we are tempted to think our suffering is worse than others, but Paul was called to suffer. In Acts 9:16, God says, *"I will show him how many things he must suffer for My name's sake."* How would you like that to be your calling? I would be tempted to leave that call unanswered, but Paul did indeed suffer for his faith in Christ. In 2 Corinthians 11:22–33, he even listed the "many things" he suffered for Christ — not as a pity party, but as a reminder of God's strength in all seasons. Paul worked harder than others to serve the kingdom of God and what did he get for his faithfulness? Imprisonments, shipwrecks, sleepless nights, floggings, whippings, beatings with rods, pelting with stones, lying cold and naked without food or water, and finally, one daring escape from government authorities by being lowered in a basket from a window. Phew! And still, Paul wrote 2 Corinthians about how we can win.

Paul had much to grieve, but in seeing the strength of God in his struggles, it became good grief. He won. It would be wonderful if we were never sad, never had any suffering, but this is not heaven. This is not our home (Hebrews 13:14). Yet without suffering, we would not grow either. We would never develop our faith. We would never know what it is to be led in the triumph of Christ through our sufferings.

Do you realize that some of the areas where God will be the most powerful to you are in the areas you lack?

After all, how will you ever know God as a provider if you never struggle financially? How will you ever know God as healer if you are never sick? How will you ever know God as strong and faithful until you see what else and who else does not hold up? It is our trials that show us God's power! It is our trials that show us God's beauty. God is always powerful, always beautiful, but it is when our earthly needs falter and fade that heaven shines all the brighter.

SCARS INTO STARS

Paul's greatest credentials were in his scars and his stars. Sometimes we only want to show our stars, sharing nothing but our successes, but what about our failures? What about the hardships that left a scar? We can grieve over our foolishness — still shaking our heads over what we did long ago — but I have found that when you are stupid, God loves you anyway. When I read about Paul's scars, I realized those are really his stars. No question about it. We must learn to see our scars as stars.

When I first ministered to Muslims, I was invited to Egypt. Everything was new to me, and I did not know what I was doing. I was told to bring the money to cover the broadcast costs, and I excitedly gave it to the government as soon as I landed in Egypt. When the technician arrived the next day, he said, "Don't give the money to the government until after. They won't do your broadcast otherwise." When I confessed what I had done, he replied, "How could you be such an idiot? Now they'll never do it."

I remained hopeful. "I believe God helps idiots," I said. "I believe we'll get it done," and I prayed to the God Most High.

> **It would be wonderful if we were never sad, never had any suffering, but this is not heaven.**

A connection from the Egyptian parliament joined us and he warned, "Don't tell anyone I said this, but do not give the government the money first, because if you do, they will never do the broadcast." Again, I confessed, and he replied, "How could you be so stupid? They probably won't broadcast now."

I still replied, "I know that was stupid and I know I did the wrong thing, but I believe God will do it," and again, I prayed to the God Most High.

This man from the Egyptian parliament put in a phone call to a woman with high connections, Jehan Sadat. Jehan Sadat was the widow of the late Egyptian President, Anwar Sadat (who was assassinated the previous year), and she led the way for civil rights reformations. It was my mistake that allowed me to meet her at her mansion. It was a pleasant experience, sipping tea next to the Nile River, and it is a memory I still smile about today, but can you guess what she told me? Yup. I had to tell her I had already given over the money. Can you guess how she replied? Yes, stupid, got it. Now I had three witnesses all calling me an idiot. This was beginning to look like something I would always regret, but Jehan Sadat made her phone call, and I prayed to the God Most High.

That call did it! The broadcast went out and my ministry to Muslims rapidly increased from this foolish start. You can call me stupid, you can make me suffer, but if I can do what God has called me to do, the suffering is worth it. This is a story I love to tell because God transformed my shame into shining glory. You do not know everything, but God does. Take Jesus into your stupidity and He will help you through. With God, my scar became a star. Yours can, too.

BAD CIRCUMSTANCES REQUIRE GOOD GRIEF

God can make you victorious in suffering. You can come out thinking it was all worth it, but you must make the choice as to whether this will be good grief that brings life or bad grief that brings destruction. Part of why it is so easy to choose bad grief is because it makes sense to the natural mind. You see destruction and continue to choose destruction, but God's ways are not our ways (Isaiah 55:8–9). When destruction comes your way, you must go God's life-giving way. We must not face our trials with natural responses but with supernatural leading. It is the only way to win.

> When you are stupid, God loves you anyway.

There is a story Corrie ten Boom tells in her autobiography, *The Hiding Place,* that I will always remember. It is the story everyone remembers because she wrote of facing grief God's way in one of her darkest trials. Corrie was in Germany in 1947. This was only two years after the end of the Second World War, and she came to preach to that defeated, bombed-out country the message that God forgives. This was not a naïve belief. Corrie ten Boom had lost deeply during that war. She had much to grieve. Both she and her sister, Betsie, were arrested and sent to a concentration camp for hiding Jewish people in their home in Haarlem, Netherlands. Their father was arrested, too, and he died in prison 11 days later. Amazingly, at the time the ten Booms were arrested, the six Jews hiding in the secret room of their house were not discovered and all survived. Instead, starving and frail, Betsie ten Boom died in the Ravensbrück concentration camp in Germany.

After her sermon in Germany in 1947, Corrie stood face-to-face with a prison guard from Ravensbrück. He had come to church to hear her speak. This was the first time since her release that she stood across from one of her captors. Though free, Corrie ten Boom's body remembered the terrors of captivity. She froze when this former guard told her that he had become a Christian. He believed God forgave the cruel things he did in the Nazi camp, but he wanted to know, especially after her message, would Corrie forgive him, too?

Corrie ten Boom said she knew that forgiveness is not an emotion but an act of will. She also knew the final warning of the parable of the unmerciful servant. She recalled what Jesus told Peter when he asked how often he should forgive. She had seen the difference between those who stayed bitter and those who got better:

> I knew (forgiveness) not only as
> a commandment of God, but as a daily
> experience. Since the end of the war I had had
> a home in Holland for victims of Nazi brutality.
>
> Those who were able to forgive their former
> enemies were able also to return to the
> outside world and rebuild their lives, no
> matter what the physical scars. Those who
> nursed their bitterness remained invalids.
> It was as simple and as horrible as that.

Hear this beautiful truth from the ugliest of circumstances: You can naturally nurse your bitterness, or you can supernaturally forgive. You can be bitter or you can get better. Where do you think God brings His healing?

Corrie ten Boom said shaking the Nazi guard's hand was the most difficult thing she ever had to do, but she knew she had to do it. She prayed silently, "Jesus, help me! . . . I can lift my hand. I can do that much. You supply the feeling." She extended her hand of forgiveness to the Nazi guard, and do you know what happened when he shook it? She describes feeling the power of God racing down her arm into their joined hands. She felt a healing warmth all over her body. This comfort broke her. She spoke out genuine forgiveness to the Nazi guard from her faithful obedience.

You can be bitter or you can get better.

Why did God not *first* send Corrie ten Boom the power to shake the offender's hand? Why did the power of the Holy Spirit only come *after* she extended her hand in forgiveness? Because she needed to choose for this to be good grief. It is when we choose to live God's way that we encounter the triumph of Christ, and it becomes our own. We can extend our hands to forgive, we can choose our words, but it is God who moves through us to make it real.

Just like forgiveness, faithfulness is not an emotion, but an act of will. Every last one of us will face suffering, but every last one of us has the free will to decide how we will suffer. We were created that way. We can choose.

JESUS CARRIES BOTH OUR SINS AND SORROWS

We often quote Isaiah 53:5 — I have already done so in this book — but read it with the previous verse:

Surely He has borne our griefs
And carried our sorrows;
Yet we esteemed Him stricken,
Smitten by God, and afflicted.
But He was wounded for our transgressions,
He was bruised for our iniquities;
The chastisement for our peace was upon Him,
And by His stripes we are healed.

ISAIAH 53:4–5

Do you see that Jesus not only took your sins, but He also took your griefs and your sorrows? That is a beautiful scripture. Sometimes I find it easier to give Jesus my sins than my grief and sorrow. I give them, but I am quick to take them back. I leave sin with Christ — after all, He paid for it — but I struggle to leave my grief and sorrow there. I pick them up again the next morning. Yet when I repent of sins, I often do not want to pick those up again. What if the blood of Jesus cleanses grief and sorrow, too? Here is where your choice to live in faithfulness comes in. If I can have faith for Jesus to forgive my sins, can I also believe that He can take my sorrow and grief?

I saw this when my father died. My mother kept on grieving. Grief is a healthy process; I thank God for it, but my mother carried her grief for far too long. A year in, it seemed as though her grief had not progressed. There was no process. Her grieving was stuck. *She* was stuck. The Lord really dealt with me. I understood the commandment to weep with those who weep (Romans 12:15), I understood the need to care for my mother, but I also sensed the need to correct her. It was hard for me to call my mother and talk to her about this because she was older in the Lord. She was the one who guided me in spiritual ways. I did not know what God would do, but I knew that I could call.

I asked my mother, "Do you believe that Jesus carried your sins?"

She said, "You know I believe that."

I said, "Well, do you believe He also carried your griefs and sorrows?"

She hesitated. She said, "I know what you're going to say. You're going to say I'm carrying them."

"Yes," I said, "and we need to pray that you would let them go and let Jesus carry them." My mother loved to pray, so this was the way to bring her grief and sorrow to Jesus. She let them go into the hope and trusted care of almighty Jesus, and she no longer carried the grief and sorrow of my father's death. She made the choice to walk in faith.

You may say your grief is not so easily ended, but in knowing my own failings in this area, I will ask you again: Are you leaving your grief and sorrow with Jesus? What would it look like to give them to Him again and to finally leave them there?

MY TURN TO GRIEVE

You have turned for me my mourning into dancing;
You have put off my sackcloth and clothed
*   me with gladness,*
To the end that my glory may sing praise to
*   You and not be silent.*
O Lord my God, I will give thanks to You forever.
PSALM 30:11–12

After almost 58 years of marriage, my husband, Wally, died in 2012. We never got to see our diamond anniversary and the years do not feel the same without him. The Christmas before he died, I was invited to preach in Bethlehem on Christmas Day. That is the kind of appointment I have prayed for my whole life, but I could not go. I was too worn down. Our anniversary was December 26, and I wondered how many more we would have.

Just like forgiveness, faithfulness is not an emotion, but an act of will.

We did not get another anniversary. Wally died the following October. I did not just grieve the loss of my husband; I grieved the loss of my ministry partner, but I knew I needed to grieve well. I knew the loss of my good marriage needed to be good grief. Because of Jesus, I know good can come from death. It was still hard, but I chose to let Jesus carry my grief and sorrow the best I could. That night, I woke up singing in tongues. I have experienced many moves of the Holy Spirit, but never this! I asked the Lord what this was, and He said, "Because I danced over you last night."

Zephaniah 3:18 says that God gathers those who sorrow. The previous verse says that God *"will quiet you with His love, He will rejoice over you with singing"* (Zephaniah 3:17). I did not know that my spirit would sing back.

After this, my grief and sorrow eased. Jesus carried them in a way I never expected. Sure enough, God had the right comfort for me in the loss of my husband. He made it beautiful in its time.

DIFFERENT KINDS OF GRIEF

Grief is not just for the death of a loved one. It can be the death of a relationship, the death of a dream, something that you wanted to do all your life. We experience many little deaths in our lives, but God is always raising us to life. Whatever the burden, God comforts the downcast (2 Corinthians 7:6). Yet if we never acknowledge we are grieving, we cannot make it good grief. If you do not deal with grief, sooner or later, it will steal your happiness, your health, your success, your ministry, or even your life.

King Solomon in all his wisdom knew we needed to face the reality of death and grieving. In Ecclesiastes 7:3 he wrote, *"Sorrow is better than laughter, for by a sad countenance the heart is made better."* I want to laugh every day, unburdened by life's sorrows. I love to rejoice in the Lord, but sometimes it is by facing sorrow that our hearts are made better.

So, I will ask you, is there anything in your life you are grieving? Do you need to finally admit your hurts and disappointments? No need to overdo it, but do not cover your grief. If Jesus talked about His sufferings, you should talk about yours, too. Take it to Him. He can carry your sorrows as well as your sins.

Now I will ask, if you know you are grieving, will you choose to let this grief change you for good? Sometimes we are tempted to say that our circumstances are unfair, but grace is unfair! The unfair grace of God saves us. Still, the psalmists would often complain to God about the unfairness of life, asking, "Why do the wicked prosper while the righteous suffer?" (Psalm 73). God put this in His good book because He knows how we think. We wonder why we are sick and why our family faces certain trials, while those who care nothing about God seem happy and healthy and thriving. We wonder why God-given dreams never became reality.

We *must* grieve with God for our hearts to get better. Ignoring it won't help. Sometimes you need to cry. Sometimes you need to choose to get up from your grief and get happy anyway. After all, as Ecclesiastes 3:1 says, there is *"a time for every purpose under heaven."* This is why we let the Holy Spirit lead us, because He knows what we truly need today, and when He makes it beautiful in its time, your grief will end. Do you know this? Your grief will end.

Whatever the burden, God comforts the downcast.

Good grief allows us to say goodbye to something we lost so that we can say hello to something new. Let me give you an example: I know many people who wanted to get married but never married, many who wanted children but never had children. There came a time when they had to grieve the loss of the life they would never live. There came a time to say goodbye, and some of these people became so gracious to lonely adults and lonely children. They were satisfied in the new that God gave them.

You can look to new beginnings. At the end of all things, Revelation 21:4–5 says, *"God will wipe away every tear from their eyes; there shall be no more death, nor sorrow, nor crying. There shall be no more pain, for the former things have passed away. Then He who sat on the throne said, 'Behold, I make all things new.' And He said to me, 'Write, for these words are true and faithful.'"*

Does this sound familiar? Paul, in seeing victory over his suffering, made a similar declaration in 2 Corinthians 5:17, *"Therefore, if anyone is in Christ, he is a new creation; old things have passed away; behold, all things have become new."* When God says, "Behold," He wants you to pay attention, and what does God call our attention to? Him making *all* things new.

I sat with this verse in Revelation 21:5 for years. I would pray, "God, this is a horrible mess, but you said you make all things new." I wrote down this Scripture every day for a year because of what it says in Habakkuk 2:2: *"Write the vision and make it plain on tablets, that he may run who reads it."* I was tired of the disappointment over what fell apart and what never came to be. I wanted to run when I felt stuck, so I kept writing the vision of Revelation 21:5.

I was not ready to behold the new when Wally passed, but over time, I chose to let God make my heart better. Over the years, I have encouraged people that they need to sow into God's kingdom to reap its benefits. For this reason, when Wally died, I sowed his life insurance money into the ministry. This way, we could partner together one more time. Since I gave that to God, doors have opened to the Middle East that were closed for decades. I still behold the difference this decision made. I wanted to see good come from Wally's death and, one day, I hope good can come from mine. I once told a newspaper reporter I would be fine facing martyrdom. "Why waste your death?" I said. "A lot of people get saved by martyrs." But I am still here. I cannot waste my life either.

In my final years, I still aim for faithfulness. That's what Paul told us to do, saying, *"We make it our aim, whether present or absent, to be well pleasing to Him. For we must all appear before the judgment seat of Christ, that each one may receive the things done in the body, according to what he has done, whether good or bad"* (2 Corinthians 5:9–10). This is why I tell everybody, "This is the best day of my life, because Jesus Christ lives big in me today!" If you get faith in your day, who knows what good God can do, even in your grief.

Grief will be productive one way or another. It will produce death, or it will produce life. In response, you can choose bad grief or you can choose good grief. Choose wisely.

Therefore, if anyone is in Christ, he is

a new creation; old things have passed away;

behold, all things have become new.

2 CORINTHIANS 5:17

We make it our aim, whether present or absent, to be well pleasing to Him. For we must all appear before the judgment seat of Christ, that each one may receive the things done in the body, according to what he has done, whether good or bad.

2 CORINTHIANS 5:9–10

CHAPTER FIVE

POWER TO OVERCOME ANXIETY

"Therefore do not worry, saying, 'What shall we eat?' or 'What shall we drink?' or 'What shall we wear?' For after all these things the Gentiles seek. For your heavenly Father knows that you need all these things. But seek first the kingdom of God and His righteousness, and all these things shall be added to you. Therefore do not worry about tomorrow, for tomorrow will worry about its own things. Sufficient for the day is its own trouble."

MATTHEW 6:31–34

In getting older, I realize that there are things I will never do again. Some are good and I miss them. I lament that I will not *get to* do them again. Others are bad and I do not miss them at all. I am glad that I do not *have to* do them again, but at some point, you realize that much of what you used to do will not come around again. You never even realized it was the last time when it happened.

I look back on old photographs and I see clothes I no longer wear, people I no longer know, and places I no longer go. Sure enough, I did not know it would be the last time then. These days I try to realize that whatever I am doing, this could be the last time. This helps me live well. Where I used to see worry, now I see opportunity. Whether good or bad, God still has me here, and I thank Him for what I have today.

I never liked roller coasters. There was no first or last time for me. No, thank you. Life feels like enough of a roller coaster as it is. The slow rises, the fast drops, all the ups and downs, then a very sudden stop. I get that experience for free. In the previous chapters, I wrote about long seasons of suffering, then seasons of outright grief, but sometimes life is volatile. You have ups and downs, joys and struggles, and back and forth you go. As Proverbs 24:16 says, the righteous may fall seven times, but they rise again. Your life may be a little roller coaster with little ups and downs. It may be a big roller coaster with extreme ups and extreme downs. You may face long falls, but also big pick-ups, yet it is through these changes that you learn to hold on to our unchanging God. You see His desire to pick you up and get you through.

Sometimes life feels like many different roller coasters all going at once. One part of your life goes up while another goes down. You get sick, you get healthy, then your spouse gets sick. One child comes out of a tough season, only for another child to face a difficult situation. Things go well at home, then you struggle at work, then they flip. You wonder, *Why can't all of life be good at the same time?* But the Bible reminds us that *"the world is passing away"* (1 John 2:17). Soon, we can find ourselves worrying about what *could* be. I do not have to explain how disgusting anxiety is. It affects the young and the old. Anxiety tempts you to take your eyes off God and turn them to your worries.

You might not know where to look during the confusion anxiety can bring, but Jesus speaks to our worries with the one action we should take: *"Seek first the kingdom of God and His righteousness"* (Matthew 6:33). He says that when we seek what God cares about, our needs will be met. I find that fascinating. For all we can worry about, Jesus gives just one instruction: Seek. You may be worn out, you may face uncertainty about the future, but you can still choose to seek Jesus' rule over your life.

Likewise, the apostle Paul penned the letter to the Philippians late in his life. Although imprisoned, he wrote of joy and how to face anxiety:

> *Be anxious for nothing, but in everything by prayer and supplication, with thanksgiving, let your requests be made known to God; and the peace of God, which surpasses all understanding, will guard your hearts and minds through Christ Jesus.*
> PHILIPPIANS 4:6–7

What should you be anxious about? Nothing. And what should you bring to God? Everything. No matter what you might face, the Bible again gives one clear instruction: Bring your worries to God with thankfulness. Paul gave thanks in prison! Even people outside of the church are learning about the power of thankfulness. Thankfulness improves your resilience, your relationships, your long-term mental health, and even your physical health. God made us to live thankful. You can place anything and everything you face within the Alpha and Omega, Jesus Christ (Revelation 22:13). You might not even understand how it happens, but when you make your requests known to God with thanksgiving, He guards your heart and mind. That is some serious security!

After several years of pastoring, we changed the name of our church. Actually, the name was chosen for us. People would faithfully come on Sunday nights and God would faithfully show up. There was so much laughter, healing, and joy that people would say, "Let's go to that happy church," and so that was what we were called: Happy Church. This will not surprise you, but we were not always happy. However, this is key: We *tried* to be. No matter the circumstance, we would lift our eyes back up to Jesus' kingdom with thanksgiving.

God knows all your days. He sees ahead because He is Jehovah-Jireh. Jehovah-Jireh does not simply mean "The Lord will provide." Jehovah-Jireh is a reminder that God is the one who sees ahead. He *knows* the ups and downs of your life, so He knows how to provide. Before you ever dropped into a slump or rose up in victory, God said,

"I've already been here. I'm here to pick you up out of this." No matter how far or numerous the falls, God has prepared bigger pick-ups to lift you out.

What Hebrews 4:12 says is true: *"For the word of God is living and powerful, and sharper than any two-edged sword, piercing even to the division of soul and spirit, and of joints and marrow, and is a discerner of the thoughts and intents of the heart."* Your circumstances may change, your thoughts and heart may change, but God speaks piercing and powerful truth to all the changes life can bring. Whether we are calm or anxious, we learn how to ask, "What are you saying today, Lord?" and He teaches us how to listen.

EXCELLENT POWER IN NORMAL PEOPLE

While seeking and thankfulness are great pathways out of worry and anxiety, God also gives believers power to stand and fight.

Second Corinthians 4 is a great chapter for facing change. It gives you the key to understanding what God can do in your life through all the ups and downs. Verse 7 says, *"We have this treasure in earthen vessels, that the excellence of the power may be of God and not of us."* This means every born-again believer has the treasure of the gospel inside of them. You may say, "I know what I think and feel inside. I know I blow it." We all do, because we are earthen vessels, but God has His treasure in us. What is that treasure? It is power from God. This power is not from us because we are earthly, but we have a treasure of power inside of us. Is this weak power or mediocre power? No, God's power is excellent power. Just because this power does not look like what you see in others does not make the power God gave you less valuable. This is God-given treasure! Every Christian has excellent power.

> **Before you ever dropped into a slump or rose up in victory, God said, "I've already been here. I'm here to pick you up out of this."**

There are three or four kinds of power described in the Greek New Testament. Let's look at two of them. There is *exousia*, which is authority power. The crowds in Jesus' day were amazed because He taught with authority (Matthew 7:29) and He gave that same *exousia* to His disciples to drive out unclean spirits (Mark 6:7).

When you pray God's Word, you are praying in God's authoritative power.

My husband, Wally, knew that God cares deeply about the poor and expects Christians to join in (Isaiah 58:10–11). One year, Wally sensed that we should double our giving to missionaries working with the poor. This giving was above our normal tithing, but we thought, *Let's go for it*. So, we gave double. Ten days later at a prayer meeting, someone gave us $10,000. Like I do when anyone gives any amount to the ministry, I gave thanks.

Every born-again believer has the treasure of the gospel inside of them.

I thought of how this amount could best be used to serve and grow what God was doing, but the man interrupted. "No," he said, "this is for you personally." I had never seen that happen. This was the exact amount of our additional giving to missions. I fully believe that, without being obedient to give, we would not have released God's power in our finances in that way. Obedience to God's Word brings God's authoritative power.

Next, there is also *dunamis*, which is miracle-working power. This is the power Jesus used to heal (Luke 5:17) and this is the same *dunamis* the Holy Spirit gave to the early church (Acts 4:33; 8:13). This same miracle-working power is in every Christian. When you look at suffering, you will see that there is a power with suffering, and it is not *exousia*. It is actually *dunamis*. So, in a suffering time, there is an opportunity for God to reveal His miracle-working power to you.

Some parts of the world are so hardened to the gospel that God chooses to move in excellent power. God speaks to them authoritatively in dreams and He speaks to them in miraculous healings. I have stood before audiences at Muslim conferences and my anxiety kicked in. I thought, *Oh God, what if nobody is healed? What if no blind eyes are open? What if nobody gets out of a wheelchair?* But I have to remind myself that I am not relying on my power. I am relying on God's excellent power. No one is healed in my name, but in Jesus' name. Who am I? I am just a little girl from Dalhart, Texas, an earthen vessel whom God took all over the world. I just say to Him, "Jesus, show up and show off."

I went to a healing conference in Amman, the capital of Jordan. I could tell by how some were dressed that these were committed Muslims. I had a dedicated team, there were Christians in the audience, and all of us earthen vessels had the same excellence of power. We planned to lay hands on the sick and to see God move. All of us looked to Jesus to see His excellent miracle-working power. It was the last night, but it seems like, invariably, God saves the best till last. A woman, dressed in black, head covered, came forward to share her testimony. She was blind in one eye for three years, but at this conference, God opened her eye and restored her sight. God healed her, and when the altar call was given, her two daughters also came forward for salvation. This was not the power of Marilyn Hickey or even the entire Christian team. This was the excellent power of the one true God.

This excellent power allows us to face all the ups and downs of life. Look at the next verse: *"We are hard-pressed on every side, yet not crushed; we are perplexed, but not in despair; persecuted, but not forsaken; struck down, but not destroyed"* (2 Corinthians 4:8–9). Big falls are met with big pick-ups, but when does the excellent power of God show? It shows when you are hard-pressed, perplexed, persecuted, and struck down. That is when you see God's excellent power keeping you from being crushed, keeping you from despair, and how it keeps you from being forsaken or destroyed. He never leaves you. The trial may be hard, but this power prevents anxiety from winning. Circumstances may change, but God is the same yesterday, today, and forever (Hebrews 13:8). We meet the anxiety of "what if?" with the faithfulness of our God who said, *"I am the Alpha and the Omega, the Beginning and the End, says the Lord, 'who is and who was and who is to come, the Almighty'"* (Revelation 1:8).

Obedience to God's Word brings God's authoritative power.

Paul continues that we are *"always carrying about in the body the dying of the Lord Jesus, that the life of Jesus also may be manifested in our body. For we who live are always delivered to death for Jesus' sake, that the life of Jesus also may be manifested in our mortal flesh. So then death is working in us, but life in you"* (2 Corinthians 4:10–12). When we have these falls, God can show His resurrection life. Why would you ever get a miracle unless you had great need? Your great need opens God's opportunity to bring miracles. Sometimes we look at our trials and say, "This is what I was afraid of," but God says, "This is what I've been waiting for to show my glory."

CONNECT TO THE POWER SOURCE

People ask me what my favorite book of the Bible is, and my husband used to answer for me, saying, "It's whatever book she's reading now." It is true. I love the different books of the Bible and the ways God speaks to my heart. It does not matter if I memorized a certain book of the Bible long ago; I hear God's fresh revelation through those words today. Still, there are teachings I keep coming back to over the years. One of them is that faith comes by hearing the Word (Romans 10:17). Paul says the same in 2 Corinthians 4:13–15:

> *Since we have the same spirit of faith, according to what is written, "I believed and therefore I spoke," we also believe and therefore speak, knowing that He who raised up the Lord Jesus will also raise us up with Jesus, and will present us with you. For all things are for your sakes, that grace, having spread through the many, may cause thanksgiving to abound to the glory of God.*

This is not a secret: Anybody who reads their Bible has access to faith, but you release it by believing it and speaking it. That's the spirit of faith. The spirit of faith is available for whatever we face. When the roller coaster of life goes up, we believe and we speak the Word. When the roller coaster of life goes down, we believe and we speak the Word. This is the treasure that is within you. This excellent power builds and sustains your faith.

Your great need opens God's opportunity to bring miracles.

We must learn to plug into God's power sources. Without connecting, no power flows your way. I say this because there is power in suffering, but many of us do not look for God's power there. When we go through trials, we do not realize that God's power is more available in our time of suffering than at any other time in our walk with Him. We think God's power is available when we praise, get happy, and when we experience His anointing. We love all that, but I am telling you the greatest power you see described in the Bible is in your time of suffering. If Jesus had not suffered on the cross, if He had not died, would we know resurrection? Our greatest example of God's power comes through the suffering and death of Christ. Why should we, as His followers, expect it will be any different for us?

CONTAGIOUS FAITH

Even though all Christians have God's excellent power, why do some people's treasures work better than others? It is because no matter the circumstance, no matter the result, they believe and speak the Word. How do you release the power of your faith? You believe and speak the Word. This excellent power comes from the death and resurrection of Jesus. Hebrews 12:2 tells us that Jesus endured the cross for the joy set before Him. He could see the big pick-up. Could you endure your cross? Could this help you see God, knowing there is a big pick-up coming? I would say resurrection is the biggest pick-up we will ever get, and God says it is for all of us. Every born-again Christian has a promise of tremendous resurrection coming their way.

You can benefit from getting around people with great faith. Faith is contagious. I have heard it said that "faith is more caught than taught," but I believe it is both. We should learn from what people teach, but we also learn from how people live. My son-in-law, Reece, has the same spirit of faith as I do, yet he believes and speaks for powerful provision. I remember one night at church he said to me, "You are going to get a $100,000 gift for your ministry." I thought, *Are you a crackpot?* But

I did not speak it. Why would I speak against the spirit of faith in him? Six weeks later, that $100,000 check came in. Just like 2 Corinthians 4:15 says, this was for my sake; Reece's same spirit of faith spread to me, and thanksgiving abounded to the glory of God. Now I believe and speak the Word for powerful provision.

You have got to take the same spirit of faith into every circumstance. You must take the same spirit of faith into every worry, every trial, and every high and low. Believe and speak the Word and see how God's excellent power moves through you.

SUFFERINGS ON THE SCALE

Therefore we do not lose heart. Even though our outward man is perishing, yet the inward man is being renewed day by day. For our light affliction, which is but for a moment, is working for us a far more exceeding and eternal weight of glory, while we do not look at the things which are seen, but at the things which are not seen. For the things which are seen are temporary, but the things which are not seen are eternal.

2 CORINTHIANS 4:16–18

Since we experience God's excellent power in suffering, we should not lose heart. You may say, "Well, I am getting older. I see more wrinkles, have less energy, and don't remember things like I used to." That may be true. It can seem like when you get older, everything starts to go downhill, but the Bible says that though the outward man is perishing, the inward man is a roaring lion. The inward man is going for it. Why? Because he is living in a spirit of faith.

> **God's power is more available in our time of suffering than at any other time in our walk with Him.**

I love to hear missionary stories. They inspire and encourage me to take my eyes off my light affliction and onto Christ. One such man was Don Richardson. He took his wife and seven-month-old child to the remotest islands of Indonesia to share the gospel with the Sawi tribe. What did his light affliction include? Learning a difficult language, facing disease, and living amidst warring tribes. Worse than that, the Sawi valued deceit and treachery. As a result, they believed Judas was the hero of the Gospels and that Jesus was to be laughed at. Where would you even begin? Worse still, the Sawi were cannibals. They might fatten you up with your favorite foods over months only to pull out a sword one night and kill you. A person deceived was their favorite food!

As a result of constant battles, disease, and treachery, many Sawi died before the age of 34. Not surprisingly, Don Richardson was discouraged by his light affliction, but he believed in what he called "redemptive analogies." He believed that, as Ecclesiastes 3:11 says, God has given every person a desire for eternity. There is no cannibal, Buddhist, Hindu, atheist, or backslidden Christian who does not have a desire for eternity. Every culture, even this destructive Sawi culture, has stories that speak to God's redemption. Don asked the Sawi, "Do you have a way of making peace with anybody?"

One Sawi told him of the Peace Child. They would hold a ceremony where children would be exchanged between opposing villages. This would bring peace, but one village would have to initiate by giving their child first. Right when the Richardsons were ready to leave, the Sawi decided to make peace with an enemy to convince the Richardsons to stay. One Sawi man ran up and gave his son to his enemy. Don Richardson wrote that, to the Sawi, "If a man would actually give his own son to his enemies, that man could be trusted!" He told them of John 3:16, of how our heavenly Father gave His Peace Child, Jesus Christ, to a hostile world. Entire tribes came to know Christ, responding to the eternity God had already placed in their hearts. This is how light, momentary affliction works for eternal purpose.

Still, sometimes I am tempted to say that my afflictions are not light, but Paul does not tell the reader to compare their sufferings to his or to valiant missionaries, but to the *"exceeding and eternal weight of glory."* Go on, put your sufferings on the scale and weigh them next to all your blessings in Christ, even all you could worry over and be anxious about in the future. Romans 8:18 says that they are not even worthy of comparison to what God offers. More so, these light afflictions are being put to work to reveal eternal glory. We must remain connected to our heavenly power source. If you do not stay connected every day, you may stay in your big fall and miss God's big pick-up. Let His power flow through you!

CHAPTER SIX

THE POWER OF PATIENCE

*I will look to the Lord; I will wait for the God
of my salvation; my God will hear me.*

MICAH 7:7

When it comes to being justified before God, every Christian is an overnight success. You were dead in your sins until you believed and confessed that Jesus is Lord. Just like that, you were made righteous (2 Corinthians 5:21). Yet when it comes to the process of sanctification, no Christian is an overnight success. We all go the long way. After all, Galatians 5 describes our life with the Holy Spirit as producing fruit. Have you ever seen fruit suddenly burst forth on the vine like popcorn? Of course not! Fruit grows slowly. Likewise, the fruit of the Spirit grows slowly, even faithfully. What does it include? *"The fruit of the Spirit is love, joy, peace, longsuffering, kindness, goodness, faithfulness, gentleness, self-control"* (Galatians 5:22–23).

I could write about the value of each of these, but there is that word again: longsuffering. Other versions of the Bible translate it as "patience." Just like there is unexpected power in suffering, there is also unexpected power in patience. I rarely meet people who want to learn patience, but we all benefit from the formed fruit of already being patient.

When it comes to being justified before God, every Christian is an overnight success.

No one needs to be patient with what they naturally enjoy. When everything is working well, there is no frustration, no need to hang in there and hope things get better, and no need to grow slowly. Instead, we learn to be patient from what is *not* working. But during that process, we are not simply waiting for our circumstances to change or to end. The original Greek word for long-suffering discussed in chapter one, *hypomonē*, is used for enduring, persevering, or remaining steadfast. With the fruit of patience, you are not helplessly standing still. You are pushing back against your light affliction for good. The Spirit's fruit of patience is necessary to suffer well.

Let me be clear: This is the fruit of the Holy Spirit. This is not the fruit of the person who tries hard. You cannot attain the fruit of the Spirit by human effort; you must rely on Him. He is the one who will provide His love, His joy, His peace, and yes, His patience. The Holy Spirit grows the fruit, not you. You must remain connected to the life and power *of* the Holy Spirit to experience fruit *from* the Holy Spirit.

We know to lay down anger. After all, *"The anger of a man does not achieve the righteousness of God"* (James 1:20 NASB). After the last chapter, I hope you can see why we should lay down anxiety, but we also need to lay down our impatience. You might feel forced to do this for your kids or your spouse, but you also know there is so much in the world that can make you frustrated. Sometimes it feels good, even right, to react this way, but what if God's way is better? What if choosing to lay down our impatience and frustration is actually a form of worship?

Just like there is unexpected power in suffering, there is also unexpected power in patience.

As we lay down anger, anxiety, and impatience, we are laying down the little ways we try to be God in our lives. We stop saying, "It should be this way," as we seek to live God's way in what we face. In all circumstances, we need to lay our anger, anxiety, and impatience down at His feet.

JESUS WANTS YOU TO BE GREAT

Second Corinthians 5:17 reminds us that *"if anyone is in Christ, he is a new creation; old things have passed away; behold, all things have become new."* Every Christian was transformed by Christ and every Christian is still being transformed by Christ. Look at how the apostle Paul describes our efforts in the next verses:

> *Now all things are of God, who has reconciled us to Himself through Jesus Christ, and has given us the ministry of reconciliation, that is, that God was in Christ reconciling the world to Himself, not imputing their trespasses to them, and has committed to us the word of reconciliation.*
>
> *Now then, we are ambassadors for Christ, as though God were pleading through us: we implore you on Christ's behalf, be reconciled to God.* ***For He made Him who knew no sin to be sin for us, that we might become the righteousness of God in Him.***
>
> *We then, as workers together with Him also plead with you not to receive the grace of God in vain.*
> 2 CORINTHIANS 5:18–6:1, EMPHASIS ADDED

Throughout our God-given transformation, we are not just speaking and living as ambassadors for Christ (5:20), tasked with the ministry of reconciliation (5:18), but we work together with Jesus (6:1). What a great invitation!

Do you know that Jesus wants you to be great? This shocked me, but it is true. In Mark 10:35–40, two of the disciples demanded prominent positions in Jesus' kingdom. These brothers wanted to sit on His right and His left for everyone to see. In Matthew's account of the same story, even their mother got involved. If I were Jesus, I would have said that they were out of line, but Jesus did not talk them out of being great. Instead, He redirected their efforts, saying:

> *"You know that those who are considered rulers over the Gentiles lord it over them, and their great ones exercise authority over them. Yet it shall not be so among you; but whoever desires to become great among you shall be your servant. And whoever of you desires to be first shall be slave of all. For even the Son of Man did not come to be served, but to serve, and to give His life a ransom for many."*
> MARK 10:42–45

Jesus served and suffered for many. Each of the faithful 11 disciples, including those prideful brothers, suffered for their service to Jesus. Most were martyred, but all became great through suffering. Today's disciples face the same invitation. Do you want to be great in the kingdom of heaven? Serve. Do you want to serve well?

You will need the fruit of the Spirit, and this includes patience, especially for times of suffering.

PATIENCE OF THE PAST

In facing your current season of patience, you must remember the Holy Spirit's fruit of patience in the past. When did God already come through for you? God did not just save you then ditch you. Where has He provided? How has He changed you? Be thankful and count your blessings. Remember previous seasons of enduring patience and the fruit God brought forth. Also, remember what God has done for others. Not all seasons of enduring patience are the same. Sometimes it comes with no timeframe. You do not know when it will end.

Consider Daniel in the Old Testament. He lived his life in exile and was forced to interpret dreams for the king under threat of persecution and even death. His whole life seemed to be a tough season! In Daniel 10:2, he again faced difficulty. He fasted and prayed, enduring patiently and believing that God would provide an answer.

After three weeks, an angel arrived with the answer Daniel needed, saying, *"Do not fear, Daniel, for from the first day that you set your heart to understand, and to humble yourself before your God, your words were heard; and I have come because of your words"* (Daniel 10:12). Prayer is powerful! God hears our words and heaven answers. Notice what it says though: As soon as Daniel prayed, the angel set out to answer, yet the next verse describes a spiritual battle that lasted 21 days. I wonder what would have happened if Daniel had impatiently quit praying on day 20. Patience is necessary for Godly faith to endure.

Other seasons of enduring patience come with a stressful deadline. You think, *Oh, God, if you don't come through by this time, I'm toast!* The bill is due, the prognosis is bleak, the demand is coming, and it will not be turned away. You know God is your only option, but then the answer or provision is delayed, and sometimes it keeps being delayed. How do you wait patiently during those times?

Consider Dr. David Yonggi Cho. He began his church in South Korea with five people, but it became the largest church in the world with 830,000 members at the time of his retirement in 2008. Do you think this happened without facing struggles along the way? No, the church grew from struggle! Even Dr. Yonggi Cho's family grew from struggle.

One of his sons never came to church growth conferences, but after the son was unjustly imprisoned for six months, he came out committed. He brought his wife and family along, too. Everyone was heartbroken while this son was imprisoned, but look at the fruit: in the long term, jail made him great.

> # Be thankful and count your blessings. Remember previous seasons of enduring patience and the fruit God brought forth.

My favorite miracle I heard Dr. Yonggi Cho speak on came from a tense ultimatum. He came from a Buddhist background, so when he set up his small tent church, he did so in a Buddhist area — one that was very anti-Christian. Soon the Buddhist leaders came and told him, "This area does not belong to Christians. Leave or we'll burn your tent down."

Dr. Yonggi Cho insisted, "I'm not here to hurt you. I'm here to help you."

The Buddhist leaders asked, "How can you help us?"

There was a woman that lived in the area that endured terrible physical deformities. She could not work and was forced to beg. Dr. Yonggi Cho pointed her out, saying, "We're here to heal the sick. See that woman begging on that corner over there? Jesus is going to heal her."

They thought he was a fool but said, "If Jesus heals her within 31 days, we won't burn your tent down."

Deliverance now had a deadline, but Dr. Yonggi Cho said, "Then get ready, because Jesus is going to heal her."

At the time, the church only had 15–20 people. He told them, "We really have to pray for this lady." They already believed in healing, but the threat brought the need for an urgent move of God. So, they went to the disabled woman on her street corner. They cleaned her home, they gave her food and water, they prayed over her, they fasted, they believed God for her deliverance, but nothing happened. For 30 days they prayed, but still there was no healing.

The last night before the Buddhist leadership would come to burn the tent down, Dr. Yonggi Cho had a visitation from the Lord. In this dream, he saw an ugly woman standing at the end of his bed. She had long teeth and long hair, but it was more than ugly on the outside. She said, "Why do you want to fight me? Why don't you join me?" This was a demon. In his dream, Dr. Yonggi Cho got up and said, "I'm not joining you. You're the devil.

In Jesus' name, I rebuke you!" He pulled this thing down to the floor and stomped on it. Quite a vivid dream, but seemingly just that.

The next day was day 31, the day the leaders would come to burn down his church. As he walked down the road, Dr. Yonggi Cho saw a woman walking toward him, and he thought, *Wow, that woman looks like the crippled woman, but she's walking. She looks well, so it must be the crippled woman's sister.* He greeted her, but the woman said, "Pastor, pastor, look at me! After you came to my house last night and prayed for me, I got well."

You know God is your only option.

"But I didn't come to your house and pray for you."

"Yes, you did, pastor," she said. "You came and prayed and now I'm totally healed!"

This is what I love about being Spirit-filled: God visits you in dreams and talks to you supernaturally. When Dr. Yonggi Cho had that dream and rebuked the devil, that is when God performed the miracle. This is not natural life; this is awesome, supernatural life! Instead of burning down the tent, the leaders became Christians. This was God's beautiful timing. Instead of moving his tent or getting impatient with all the days God did not respond, Dr. Yonggi Cho and his church patiently endured despite the coming threat. Since that time, much of South Korea has responded to the gospel and there are now more people who identify as Christian than Buddhist.

When writing to the Thessalonians, the apostle Paul commended their enduring patience:

> *We are bound to thank God always for you, brethren, as it is fitting, because your faith grows exceedingly, and the love of every one of you all abounds toward each other, so that we ourselves boast of you among the churches of God for your patience and faith in all your persecutions and tribulations that you endure.*
>
> 2 THESSALONIANS 1:3–4

What does Paul boast over? Their patience and faith in suffering. What was the result? Great love in the church and rapidly growing faith. Be patient. Your love and faith will grow.

THE POWER OF PATIENCE

PATIENCE BRINGS GRACE

As God's co-workers we urge you not to receive God's grace in vain. For he says,

> *"In the time of my favor I heard you,*
> *and in the day of salvation I helped you."*

I tell you, now is the time of God's favor,
now is the day of salvation.

2 CORINTHIANS 6:1–2 NIV

You may say, "Someday, I'll get out of this suffering." But God does not tell you to look at your suffering as though *someday* you'll get help. He says *now* is the time. Now is the day of salvation. Would you like to know that right now He wants to take care of your suffering? Right now, He has a plan of salvation for you. You may think, *But nothing is changing now. What does God have for me now?* God tells you what He has. He has grace.

Grace is available for your hard times. When is it available? Now. What is grace? Grace is God's supernatural ability. God has supernatural power available to you now. Likewise, now is the time of God's favor and salvation. You may think, *Wasn't I already saved?* Yes! Thank God this is true, but remember from chapter three: Salvation also means deliverance. God says, "I have deliverance available to you right now."

Many times, we do not see this deliverance with our eyes instantly; we do not feel it. We do not smell that winning fragrance. We do not taste or even touch it because we do not realize His deliverance is here *now*. God could be comforting and strengthening you at this very second, except you are putting Him off. Do not put God off! He is available now. We have faith from what God did in the past, we have faith for what He will do in the future, but we need to have faith now. We need to believe that right *now* we have grace for our problems and suffering.

I have been in ministry a long time. I have seen so much of what life can throw at you, but I have also seen a fraction of the infinite grace God can offer. It has meant everything to me. Oh, how I never tire of God's grace!

REMAIN UNDER

Another way to translate the Greek word for longsuffering, *hypomonē*, is to "remain under." If you are always trying to get out from under suffering, you cannot receive the victory God has for you. Romans 5:3–5 tells us the result of our longsuffering:

We also glory in tribulations, knowing that tribulation produces perseverance; and perseverance, character; and character, hope. Now hope does not disappoint, because the love of God has been poured out in our hearts by the Holy Spirit who was given to us.

You might not want that patient perseverance; you might be indifferent to the character it brings, but I know you want hope that does not disappoint. If you are always trying to get out of your suffering, you cannot get the big win God is after. That is why there is power in patience. Enduring patience is necessary to obey what God has for us. If salvation calls you to be a believer, suffering calls you to be a disciple. If we take God's grace into suffering, this hope can be the greatest blessing we will ever see. We can learn to ask, "What great thing are you getting ready to do, God?"

Have you seen the fruit of people who never learned how to endure suffering? They say, "This marriage isn't working, I'll get another. This church isn't working, I'll find another. This town isn't working, I'm moving on!" They do not remain under what suffering wants to work in them. They keep on moving on when things inevitably get tough. In the end, they are some of the loneliest people you know. They are disconnected from God, and they are disconnected from people. We must patiently endure to remain connected to what God is doing.

While we patiently endure suffering, we do not sit around. There are no kingdom couch potatoes. Second Corinthians 6:1 urges you to work in God's kingdom with him. His grace is given regardless, but He wants it to bear fruit. God does not want you to waste His grace in your life. He does not want you to waste your suffering.

STAND IN THE DELAY

In traveling to many countries, I experienced many travel delays. Sometimes these delays had me standing in long lines to find a new flight; sometimes these delays had me sleeping on the airport floor until morning. While I found it frustrating that I could not start the journey I intended to take, these delays were still better than flying the wrong way. A delay in the right place is better than moving to the wrong place.

Patience is standing in the delay. You keep thinking, *I'm going to make it through this. I'm going to be triumphant in Christ. I'm going to win.* I have seen parents pray their kids and grandkids into salvation. I have seen wayward spouses come home. All these people were faithful in prayer, but for many, it took years to see gain from their pain.

If you are always trying to get out of your suffering, you cannot get the big win God is after.

It is suffering that brings prodigals home. When we read the parable of the prodigal son (Luke 15:11–32), we marvel at the father's love, but the son who ran away had that love before he left, and yet he still chose to leave. It is only after he suffered that he returned home, realizing that his father was good. Without suffering, he would have foolishly journeyed even farther from home and farther away from his good father's love.

Suffering showed me strength I never knew I had. It also showed me painful truths about my thinking that I would not have seen otherwise. Many years ago, I was sick for a year with a stomach parasite I picked up in the Middle East. I was so physically sick that I struggled to keep my mind off the pain. My stomach burned and I felt like it drove my mind crazy. I am known for being an optimistic encourager, but at this time, it was tough. I struggled to remember things, and what I could remember was negative, but I chose to work with Jesus.

Even though my body shook, I called and prayed for six sick people every day. I had no energy for long prayers, but those quick prayers took my eyes off my trials and put them onto serving with Jesus. This was how I stood with faith during the delay for that painful year. I needed that fire of transformation because I knew Jesus wanted me to be great. I remembered that, in His kingdom, greatness requires suffering. I was not going to waste my suffering. Do not waste yours.

EQUIPPED FOR SUFFERING

Second Timothy 3:16–17 teaches us that God gave us the Bible so that we would be *"thoroughly equipped for every good work,"* yet we are not just equipped by the Word but by the Holy Spirit. We are equipped with thankfulness and patient endurance in longsuffering. Second Corinthians 6:6–7 tells of some of the other equipment we are given to face suffering. We are equipped *"by purity, by knowledge, by longsuffering, by kindness, by the Holy Spirit, by sincere love, by the word of truth, by the power of God, by the armor of righteousness on the right hand and on the left."*

All this equipment is available to you now. The question is whether you will use it. A closed Bible does you no good. Living without purity, knowledge, kindness, and sincere love does you no good. Not wearing the armor of righteousness does you no good. Ignoring the Holy Spirit and doubting God's power does you no good. Live equipped.

Second Corinthians 6:8–10 reminds us that sufferings and blessings go together: *"By honor and dishonor, by evil report and good report; as deceivers, and yet true; as unknown, and yet well known; as dying, and behold we live; as chastened, and yet not killed; as sorrowful, yet always rejoicing; as poor, yet making many rich; as having nothing, and yet possessing all things."*

Sometimes I am honored; sometimes people think I am nothing. Some people say, "Marilyn Hickey? What's that, a gourmet food?" I am unknown. Even when I am known, many times, in many cultures, people have insulted me. Sometimes people think I am a deceiver; other times people think I speak truth. Yet at all times, when I receive grace and I use the equipment God gave me, I am blessed through suffering. When I am hurt, I am not killed. I am alive in Christ. When I am sad, I rejoice in the Lord. When I am poor, I am still rich in Christ. Even if I have nothing on earth, Jesus brings me to heaven.

I do not invite trials, but I welcome the fruit. Equipped with grace and patience, I always come out better. If I stick in, remain under, and let God do what He needs to do, I always come out better, not bitter. You have that same choice: Are you wasting the blessing of suffering? Are you just whining? Are you blaming God? Then you are wasting your suffering when it could be transforming you and making you great. Sometimes I have an ugly disposition while I suffer, but I have learned to look for the blessings that only come through suffering.

You are not left here to suffer and barely make it through and only get a little transformation. You will not just barely make it. God specializes in greatness. Heaven is abundant and God wants you to triumph in your suffering! Live patiently, live graciously, live equipped for every trial. Live great.

The fruit of the Spirit is love, joy, peace, longsuffering, kindness, goodness, faithfulness, gentleness, self-control.

GALATIANS 5:22–23

"Do not fear, Daniel, for from the first day that you set your heart to understand, and to humble yourself before your God, your words were heard; and I have come because of your words."

DANIEL 10:12

CHAPTER SEVEN

REPLACING STRONGHOLDS

The Lord is good, a stronghold in the day of trouble; and He knows those who trust in Him.

NAHUM 1:7

While seeking Jesus and giving thanks provide pathways to move forward through suffering, and patience allows us to endure suffering, sometimes we must fight to take back ground. The Bible calls these battlegrounds strongholds.

What are strongholds? In war, a stronghold is a fortified place designed to defend territory and to maintain rule. If you can bring down the stronghold, you can take back the whole city. Many manmade strongholds are listed throughout the Bible (Numbers 13:19; 1 Samuel 23:14; Micah 5:11). While some spiritual strongholds are of God, others are from the enemy. In spiritual warfare, a stronghold is what the devil uses to control your thoughts and turn you away from what God says is good. When it comes to a particular subject, this stronghold dominates your thinking, your emotions, and your behavior, but 2 Corinthians shows you how to win the battle:

> *Though we walk in the flesh, we do not war according to the flesh. For the weapons of our warfare are not carnal but mighty in God for pulling down strongholds, casting down arguments and every high thing that exalts itself against the knowledge of God, bringing every thought into captivity to the obedience of Christ, and being ready to punish all disobedience when your obedience is fulfilled.*
> 2 CORINTHIANS 10:3–6

Isaiah describes the devil's thought life. The devil thought, "*I will exalt my throne above the stars of God . . .*

I will be like the Most High" (Isaiah 14:13–14). The devil still tries to exalt his throne in our minds over the throne of God. Sometimes the devil uses our suffering to build negative strongholds. Often, you can control your emotions and your thoughts until that time of suffering really puts the squeeze on you. Then, when your thoughts are negative, your words become negative, and soon all you feel is negative. The devil loves this hopeless mindset. The number one thing the devil wants from you is your mind, because he can steer your life from your thoughts.

Strongholds include fears, past failures, bitterness, unforgiveness, anger, and more. A stronghold is not easily torn down. After all, it is strong, and it has a hold on your life. You cannot do this on your own. You may try to change for a little while in your fleshly efforts, but something is missing. Thankfully, you can be equipped with spiritual weapons that are *"mighty in God."* In the same way the fruit of the Spirit comes from the Holy Spirit, godly weapons are wielded by the power of God. With God, the strongholds can be pulled down and your thought life can be taken captive so Christ can rule over it. You can win!

KNOW WHERE TO FIGHT

Some strongholds are generational. You may struggle with gambling because your parents struggled with gambling and because their parents struggled with gambling and so on. Other strongholds are cultural. You might struggle with the sexual sin the world promotes. Finally, some strongholds were formed from the pain inflicted upon you. You may think, *I'll never truly be loved because of this.* But all strongholds remain undefeated when their location is shrouded in darkness. How can you win if you do not even know where to fight?

To defeat strongholds, they must first be identified. Since a stronghold is what the devil uses to control your thoughts and turn you away from what God says is good, you must look beneath the surface of your struggles. Often, we think of other people as the stronghold, saying, "If only my spouse would change" or "If only my co-worker would understand." We try to cast them down, and we seem to keep making the situation worse. Sometimes you can think of your limitations as the stronghold, saying, "If only I looked like this" or "If only my body were better." But your limitations are not the problem. Where are your thoughts negative? Is it a fear of failure, a fear of finances, a fear of the future of this country, a fear of not getting married, or a fear of the one you are already married to? Whatever your present circumstances, the real battlefield is in your mind. If the devil can keep you unaware of the real problem, he can keep you in patterns of failure.

Where is your stronghold? You need to identify it. Pray for the Holy Spirit to reveal strongholds to you. Ask your closest connections — a spouse, a close friend, your pastor, or those in your church small group — what they have seen you struggle with over the years. Then pray about the strongholds that might exist in those areas.

KNOW HOW TO FIGHT
Stop Fighting Your Way

In order to start fighting God's way, you must stop fighting your way. Your angry words are not mighty in God. Your unforgiveness, your bitterness, and you constantly getting down on yourself and others — none of these weapons are mighty in God. They are fighting the wrong battle on the wrong battleground.

Some strongholds are reinforced by what others say. We all know someone who will just keep arguing. Their words can cause you to doubt God's goodness. "How can you believe the Bible?" they say. "Oh, you believe in healing? What about this person who died believing what you're trying to believe?" They point out the sins and failures of your family as if it is the fate you will not escape. Their words become a dangerous, demonic thing.

Your mind will argue back, and your voice may follow, but the Bible tells us we cannot deal with a stronghold in this carnal way. You must deal with it the spiritual way. If you constantly push ahead based on your own thinking, you will not see what God knows will work. Despite being human, do not war according to your flesh (2 Corinthians 10:3).

Cast Down What Goes Against God

Notice where 2 Corinthians 10:4–5 describes the placement of these spiritual battles: We pull *down* strongholds. We cast *down* arguments and every *high* thing that exalts itself against the knowledge of God. These strongholds may have raised themselves up to rule over our thinking, but they are not higher than God's thinking. They cannot stand against His truth. To pull down a stronghold, we must know that it should not be up there. What should be in our mind? The knowledge of God. Part of this is knowing what God says in His Word. You cannot be spiritually minded without God's Word.

Compare your thoughts to what God says. The devil may tell you that you will not make it through these trials. Well, what does God say? *"I can do all things through Christ who strengthens me"* (Philippians 4:13). You must cast that argument down, saying, "Well, who's right, the devil or God? Only one can rule here."

If the devil can keep you unaware of the real problem, he can keep you in patterns of failure.

This verse from Philippians 4:13 has become a good stronghold for me, but this was not always the case. When I was in high school, I was terrified of public speaking class. Whenever it was time for me to speak, I was sick with nerves. I kept thinking, *I am not a public speaker* until it became a stronghold, but later, I read about what God did with Moses.

Even as God called to him from a burning bush and told him of other great things he would see, Moses set up a similar stronghold: "O *my Lord, I am not eloquent, neither before nor since You have spoken to Your servant; but I am slow of speech and slow of tongue*" (Exodus 4:10).

Although Moses declared his limitations, God declared His knowledge: *"Who has made man's mouth? Or who makes the mute, the deaf, the seeing, or the blind? Have not I, the* Lord*? Now therefore, go, and I will be with your mouth and teach you what you shall say"* (Exodus 4:11–12).

Despite being human, do not war according to your flesh.

Unlike Moses, I did not have an Aaron to help me in my public speaking class, but I knew that God made my mouth and that He could strengthen it. Still, my fear of public speaking remained a stronghold. It took years of confronting what I thought was my knowledge with God's knowledge to pull it down. Now Philippians 4:13 rules how I speak. The devil still tries to take back control, but as each fearful thought comes up, I meet it with the truth God has already used to work power in my life.

If God does not say the things you are thinking, you must get your thoughts back into the light of His Word so that the lie can be exposed and the truth can be raised up (Psalm 119:130). The apostle Paul already gave a reminder of the power of seeing clearly: *"For it is the God who commanded light to shine out of darkness, who has shone in our hearts to give the light of the knowledge of the glory of God in the face of Jesus Christ"* (2 Corinthians 4:6). The negative comes down and God's Word is exalted when you choose to believe it. See clearly where the battle truly is, then choose His Word.

Make Thoughts Obedient to Christ

To defeat a stronghold, we must not only know what the Bible says but also how to apply it. What keeps strongholds destroyed is *"bringing every thought into captivity to the obedience of Christ"* (2 Corinthians 10:5). There is a good reason why Paul says we should bring *every* thought under Christ's rule. The more thoughts are brought to Jesus, the less likely the stronghold is to return. After all, Romans 12:2 reminds us that we are transformed by the renewing of our mind.

When Jesus was tempted in the desert (Luke 4:1–13), He pulled down every lie the devil spoke using one weapon. This was not a physical weapon. Jesus wielded the Word. The Word can rout the devil, but if you do not speak it out, it will not work. Medicine cannot help if you do not take it. Even though it is designed to make you well, you must take it in. You must use it as directed. There are a lot of Christians who read the Bible but never speak it over their thought life. Because they do not speak the Word, negative thoughts are not brought captive to Christ and instead set up a stronghold. This is not how God directs us to fight. Maybe you do not know what to pray, but you can always speak the Bible over your specific situation. You can unleash the truth of the Word to battle against the lies of the enemy.

Fulfill Your Obedience

Second Corinthians 10:6 makes it clear: Warring God's way is an obedience issue. When you recognize a stronghold of the devil and know that it needs to come down, that is obedience to God. When you start using the weapon of the Word to tear down what is false, you must walk in obedience to God. Once this obedience is fulfilled, the strongholds are cast down. Any stronghold that started with your negative thinking can be the enemy's fortress to keep you defeated. That defeat can also spread to your loved ones.

When my daughter, Sarah, was in elementary school, she would cry every field day. In third grade, she told me, "I don't run well. I don't jump well. I'm just not athletic. I never win any awards." I encouraged her the best I knew how, saying, "Oh, Sarah, you're spiritual. You're so obedient and smart." Then I added, "I was never good in athletics, and you probably never will be either." My stronghold was forming a similar one in her, and I was the one helping build it. It was here I felt the Lord say to me, "Who said she can't be good in athletics? Why can't she be good at everything?" This was God-knowledge pulling on the stronghold. I did not waste what God gave me. I immediately told my daughter, "I'm wrong. I repent from telling you that."

> **You can unleash the truth of the Word to battle against the lies of the enemy.**

Once you pull a stronghold down you must replace it. Without a stronghold of God's Word in its place, the devil will try to retake that ground. In pulling down my stronghold, I wanted to pull down the stronghold in Sarah. We had three weeks until field day. I told her that we would speak the promises of God together. We had three Scriptures that we prayed every night: We prayed that she is more than a conqueror (Romans 8:37), we prayed that she always triumphs in Christ (2 Corinthians 2:14), and we prayed that she can do all things through Christ who strengthens her (Philippians 4:13). Now my God-given stronghold was building a similar one in my daughter, and I was happy to help build it along with Jesus. Then I got specific. I said, "Sarah, you're going to say every night that you will get two first place ribbons."

She replied, "But, Mom, I've never even gotten one third place ribbon." Her stronghold was still standing.

I said, "I know, but this year you're getting to first place." Every night we spoke that out with her Scriptures. On field day, all the kids were on the playground, getting ready for the competition. I went over to Sarah and asked how she was. She replied, "I'm more than a conqueror. I always triumph in Christ. I can do all things through Christ who strengthens me. Today, I get two first place ribbons." And she got them. Still today, Sarah is an athlete. She did not start out that way. She started with negative thinking, then I added more, but both of our strongholds were pulled down, and the light of God's Word replaced the lie of the devil.

SEE THE VICTORY

"Have I not commanded you? Be strong and of good courage; do not be afraid, nor be dismayed, for the LORD your God is with you wherever you go."
JOSHUA 1:9

While some strongholds are hidden and it takes time to learn where to fight, some of life's greatest strongholds are visibly powerful. We know they should not be there, but they are intimidating. We do not even know where to begin to fight. It is here we remember that some of the greatest victories in the Bible were won because people could see the victory in the spiritual realm before they saw it in the physical realm. When the giant Goliath came out to challenge the Israelites, they *"were dismayed and greatly afraid"* (1 Samuel 17:11) because they only saw the impossible physical challenge. In a contest of human strength, who could win against someone that big? Yet where others saw a physical fight, David saw a spiritual challenge to God. No man, no matter how big, will win that fight. He told Goliath, *"You come to me with a sword, with a spear, and with a javelin. But I come to you in the name of the LORD of hosts, the God of the armies of Israel, whom you have defied"* (1 Samuel 17:45). David knew it was God who would bring this victory, declaring *"that all the earth may know that there is a God in Israel"* (1 Samuel 17:46).

When God instructed the Israelites to enter the promised land, the first city they needed to conquer was Jericho. Fortified by huge walls, Jericho was the initial stronghold that guarded the rest of Canaan, but this was not the first time the Israelites were called to battle there. In Numbers 13:2, God told Moses that He was giving Canaan to the Israelites but, based on what most of the spies said, the people were too afraid to fight. They saw the physical challenge of the enemy, not the spiritual victory of God. Forty years later, the only two spies who saw God's victory before, Joshua and Caleb, were leading a young and inexperienced people out from the wilderness into battle.

This is what their physical eyes saw: *"Now the gates of Jericho were securely barred because of the Israelites. No one went out and no one came in"* (Joshua 6:1 NIV). Yet, in the very next verse, God told Joshua to view things with spiritual eyes: *"See, I have delivered Jericho into your hands, along with its king and its fighting men"* (Joshua 6:2 NIV). The Israelites had a choice: Would they see the victory God sees for them? Would they see His will making the way or the enemies' walls keeping them out?

Although inexperienced, the young Israelites grew up knowing what did *not* work. Forty years prior, it was the previous generations who would not enter the promised land when God had already declared victory. Not only did they not see this future victory, but they also questioned the past victories God had already given and instead wanted to return to slavery in Egypt (Numbers 14:1–4). Although God forgave them, their contempt kept them from seeing the promised land (Numbers 14:22–23). Seeing this warning, I will ask you: When will you grow tired of what is *not* working in your life? God says victory can be yours against strongholds. Why would you disagree?

You might not see victory over a stronghold in your life right now, but God tells you to see it how He sees it. When we get ahold of God's Word, we see what God sees rather than what we see with our natural eyes. You need to see yourself as victorious. You need to see yourself as free from fear. You need to see yourself as free from jealousy, anger, unforgiveness, ugliness, bitterness, and bad habits. These strongholds need to be torn down with spiritual weapons. Seeing God's victory before you fight the battle is key. You need to see your bills as paid each month. You need to see your marriage as sweet and loving. You need to see your children as obeying God. You need to see the victory because spiritual weapons are always faith weapons. You will never win any battle without faith, and faith comes by hearing the Word. It is the Word that commands you to see God's victory.

I have seen what replaced the city in today's Israel, but I would have loved to see God's victory come to fruition at Jericho. The Israelites did not fight with carnal weapons. They did not bring a superior military plan. They followed God's plan. God had them march around Jericho's city walls for six days. This left them open to attack, but with all things involving God, this was a trust issue. For six days, they were not to speak, but on the seventh lap of the seventh day, *"Joshua said to the people: 'Shout, for the Lord has given you the city!'"* (Joshua 6:16). The walls fell, and the stronghold of Jericho fell along with them.

This is how strongholds fall in your life, too. When you can see the victory, even before it happens, you begin to feel it. If you get into a faith mindset, your emotions will come along. They may fight you for a while, but your negative emotions will get in line. Faith is never dormant. It comes with activity, and sometimes you have to march around. Finally, there are times to be silent, but there are also times to shout. What takes the devil's stronghold down? The Word! I fully believe that if the Israelites had not shouted, those walls would not have come down. Every step of following God's plan was necessary. They had to see it, do it, and say it. You, too, have to declare the Word over your stronghold.

Seeing God's victory before you fight the battle is key.

There is always something in life that can get you down, but I have learned that if I let that negativity in, it will hold on strong until I cast it down with the Word of God. Start by finding a few promises in the Bible and speaking them over your life. The more you say these promises, the stronger they will become. Your mind will change, your emotions will change, and your actions will change. Then, when the enemy comes along, you will have a stronghold of Scripture there.

These days, I speak 30 confessions over my life every day. Life may send new problems, but they just teach me to speak new confessions. These are my strongholds now. I am equipped every day because the devil is out there to beat me to a pulp. He is chomping at the bit to get me, but cannot, because the Word overcomes sin. Even when I struggle to believe the Word, I speak it, and that starts to move my belief. Most of my 30 confessions involve joy or rejoicing in God in some way, but these confessions are one of the most effective weapons I have found. I tell the devil that "It is written," and then I tell him the Bible verse, because that's how Jesus fought His spiritual battles in Luke 4.

In Revelation 12:11, the Bible tells us of how the enemy will be defeated: *"They overcame him by the blood of the Lamb and by the word of their testimony, and they did not love their lives to the death."* Jesus has already done His work. You must tell the devil what is written in the Word, testifying to God's victory. And you must remember that your true life is the one still to come.

Decide which strongholds will be exalted in your mind — God's or the devil's. Decide who reigns there and fight with the mighty and effective spiritual weapons God has graciously given to you. See God's victory over your mind and watch your life change!

CHAPTER EIGHT

BLESSED THORNS

We know that all things work together for good to those who love God, to those who are the called according to His purpose.

ROMANS 8:28

In chapter seven, I wrote on the battleground of your mind, but this is not the only place the devil attacks. While you should get your mind right, this does not remove the pain of life's challenges or totally stop the way Satan uses your earthly struggles against you. We must again turn our eyes back to the triumph of Christ that we only see through suffering. We must see that while a thorn in the flesh is sent by the devil, it can be used by God for good.

What is a thorn in the flesh? It is not made for your spirit. It is pain that sticks in your life. We face many pains in our flesh. We believe the thorn is this person, this sickness, or this financial problem. There is a whole list of what can go wrong in life. This thorn can stick with you for a long time, and it feels like you cannot get free, but one of the wonderful things about walking with the Lord over your lifetime is that you learn that God does not just set you free, He keeps you free. After all, *"Where the Spirit of the Lord is, there is freedom"* (2 Corinthians 3:17 NIV).

I had a thorn in my flesh starting at 11 years old. I wrote about this in my autobiography, but when my family moved in with my aunt and uncle in Pennsylvania, my uncle began sexually abusing me. To everyone else, he was the nicest man they knew, and they had no clue what was happening. Even I did not understand what was happening. I did not understand the shame and confusion or the blame I put on myself. I thought there was something terribly wrong with me that caused the abuse. My uncle was never caught, and I never had the opportunity to confront him, but I did forgive him. When we moved out of his house, the abuse stopped, but I lived with the effects of that thorn. I fell into depression, and thoughts of suicide filled my mind. I constantly read about it and even tried to end my life. I felt like God had abandoned and forsaken me. No child should feel so alone.

> **While a thorn in the flesh is sent by the devil, it can be used by God for good.**

The thorn was in my flesh, but the devil was using it. Little did I know, God was redeeming it. In seventh grade, I began to do well at school and the encouragement I received lifted me out of my depression. I experienced a level of healing there, but I always felt like I had to perform and be better than everyone else because I did not feel like I could trust God. I thought that I could only rely on myself. That is the thing about a thorn — it keeps pain in the middle of what is good. Even when you try to get better, it still finds a way to hurt.

As the years went by, I completely blocked out the memories of my sexual abuse. In some ways this was useful, but I was not completely healed. It was not until

60 years later that I would truly be set free. I mentioned being sick with a parasite in chapter six. What I did not mention is that this was the way I received healing from my earlier thorn. For nine months, the doctors did not know what was wrong with me. No one had answers to my symptoms. I needed medication to be awake and medication to sleep. I dropped 20 pounds, and for my frame, that was a real problem. I was constantly sick, constantly shaking, constantly hopeless. My life was all dark clouds. I had to cancel all my trips and speaking visits. Even when I pushed through to still pray for people, on every level, I could not perform as the Marilyn Hickey people had come to know. Once again, in my 70s, I did not want to live. By the time the problem was correctly identified, I was long since worn out.

God does not just set you free, He keeps you free.

In the same way the right doctor recognized the parasite, my faith counselor friends recognized my depression. They came to my home to pray for me. They asked that the Holy Spirit would bring to mind anything I should know. It was here I remembered what my uncle had done. It was here that God reminded me that I had also thought of ending my life for a whole year when I was young. Then He spoke to how I thought He had forsaken me: "You thought I abandoned you, but I was there the whole time."

God showed me His grace over the years. He showed me how He delivered me from the abuse when my family moved out of my uncle's house. He showed me how He helped me move to the top of the class in junior high. He showed me all the people who stepped in to build me up. I had known God's faithfulness in all the good in my life, but here He showed me His faithfulness in the bad. This time of prayer not only changed my life, but it changed my view of my life so far. My heart was healed, and my joy returned. I cried for three days in the renewed hope of wanting to live. Often, we do not even know the depths of the healing we need.

You could say, "But why did it take 60 years? Why did it have to happen at all?" I do not have all the answers, but I know the goodness of God can heal the darkest suffering. No matter your thorn, no matter how long it has hurt, it is never too late to experience the healing power of Jesus in your life.

THORNS HAVE PURPOSE

While my longsuffering had an end and my thorn was removed, the apostle Paul experienced the grace of God in a different way. At the start of 2 Corinthians 12, Paul describes a man who experienced an incredible vision and revelation from God. This man was *"caught up into Paradise"* (12:4). It is likely Paul was this man, but he shared this experience from 14 years earlier reluctantly (12:2). Paul was reluctant because others in the church would boast in how special they were to receive visions of God. Instead, Paul wrote, *"I will not boast, except in my infirmities"* (12:5). Why would Paul instead boast in physical or mental weakness?

> No matter your thorn, no matter how long it has hurt, it is never too late to experience the healing power of Jesus in your life.

At the start of chapter four, I noted Paul's list of sufferings in 2 Corinthians 11:21–33. Near the end of his list of suffering, he concludes, *"If I have to boast, I will boast of what pertains to my weakness"* (2 Corinthians

11:30 NASB). Again, why would Paul want to boast about weakness? The answer is here in chapter 12:

> *Lest I should be exalted above measure by the abundance of the revelations, a thorn in the flesh was given to me, a messenger of Satan to buffet me, lest I be exalted above measure. Concerning this thing I pleaded with the Lord three times that it might depart from me. And He said to me, "My grace is sufficient for you, for My strength is made perfect in weakness." Therefore most gladly I will rather boast in my infirmities, that the power of Christ may rest upon me. Therefore I take pleasure in infirmities, in reproaches, in needs, in persecutions, in distresses, for Christ's sake. For when I am weak, then I am strong.*
>
> 2 CORINTHIANS 12:7–10

Nobody had a life with God like Paul. He was not just called to suffer for Christ but to experience Him mightily. The two experiences are closely tied. Paul could have easily thought highly of himself based on all the revelation God gave him, but here we learn the thorn had a purpose. While the devil had purpose in Paul's thorn to limit his usefulness, God's purpose in Paul's thorn was to keep him from becoming prideful. You may think, *I could be so much more effective if I didn't have this thorn! My ministry would be so much better without these limitations!* Yet God disagrees. We have all met prideful Christians. We have all met humble Christians. Which one do you prefer? Which one do you think has experienced more of God's purpose in their thorns? It may feel like these thorns are breaking you down, but brokenness makes room for God.

Paul was clear though: This thorn was a messenger of Satan. It hurt. A buffet may mean a lot of food to most people, but "to buffet" someone means to hit or knock them off course. We all know what it feels like when the hits of life keep coming. Your thorns buffet you mercilessly. No wonder Paul pleaded that this thorn would depart from him. It was from Satan, but God used it. God said no to Paul's prayer like He sometimes says no to our prayers. There is more going on than we know.

What was Paul's thorn anyway? Some say his thorn was a physical ailment. It would be harder to minister if your eyesight or speech was affected. Some say it was a sinful temptation, while others believe the thorn referred to a difficult person. The Old Testament does describe some people as being a thorn in the side (Numbers 33:55; Joshua 23:13).

My theory is that Paul's thorn was the Jews who persecuted him. He longed to see them saved (Romans 10:1), but they kept hitting him with whips and rods and stones. Even when buffeted harshly, Paul had a heart for people. Sometimes it is the people we love the most who hurt us the most.

> It may feel like these thorns are breaking you down, but brokenness makes room for God.

I am convinced of my theory! I have preached in depth on this with more evidence, but here is the truth: The Bible does not tell us Paul's thorn. We do not need to know. If we did know, it would not help. We might even dismiss it because it is not the thorn we face. Instead, what Paul wrote about his unknown thorn is what we need to know about our thorns.

Thorns still feel disgusting to me, but I put my hand on my heart and I say, "I won't forget that while the thorn in the flesh comes from Satan, it is used by God." Even when it hurts, I still want what God is after in my life.

The devil does not realize that he is really God's errand boy. Remember, it was the devil who set up Christ's crucifixion, and without it, there would be no forgiveness of sins and no resurrection. This was not what he had in mind, but God used it. So, can God use your thorn in the flesh even though it comes from Satan? Can God use your harsh spouse, your rebellious child, or your troubled past? Can He use your illness, your loneliness, or your reoccurring financial strain? Whatever your thorn, God can use it. He might not choose to take your thorn away, but He will add grace. God's grace was sufficient for Paul's thorn, and it is enough for yours.

While the thorn in the flesh comes from Satan, it is used by God.

This is the part that really bothers me: When I read 2 Corinthians 12:10, oh, does it bother me. Paul wrote that he took *"pleasure in infirmities, in reproaches, in needs, in persecutions, in distresses, for Christ's sake."* I do not take pleasure in these most of the time, but I am learning that when you take pleasure in these thorns, God will provide His power. The pleasure is in knowing that your suffering is being used for Christ's sake. If suffering will happen in my life anyway, I want it to be for His glory.

JESUS SEEKS THE WEAK

This is one of my favorite topics to speak about: God is attracted to weakness. Not the strong in the world, but the weak. Read the Gospels. Who did Jesus side with: the sick or the healthy, the poor or the rich, the honest sinner or the proud Pharisee? Every time in every story, Jesus backs the weak.

I have lived life trying to be strong in my own efforts, and I have lived life learning to be weak in Christ. Weak is better because it is where Jesus is. Do not misunderstand; I want a strong prayer life. I want to be strong in the Word. I want to be strong for others, but I know my limits. They show me that I am not the god of my life. Sometimes I feel weak in my body and weak in my mind. Sometimes I do not feel like I have the prayer life I want or the revelation I need. Good! It is then that I more deeply feel the need for the Holy Spirit to guide me.

How do you get strong when you are weak? By acknowledging your weakness and relying on God.

I once flew to a healing meeting in Ukraine. This was soon after the Iron Curtain fell in the early 90s, and suddenly there were opportunities to minister that were not there before. After 22 hours on a plane and jetlag to boot, I just wanted to go to bed, but the students driving us to the hotel asked, "Would you mind praying for this demon-possessed girl?" I did mind! I felt as spiritual as a frog. "Can't we just do it tomorrow?" I asked, but they insisted. They were witnessing on the street, and this girl might not be there again. Still, I resisted. I thought, *They're just students. This girl probably has a cold and they're exaggerating*, but I asked, "How do you know she's demon possessed?"

If suffering will happen in my life anyway, I want it to be for His glory.

They told me that this 17-year-old, Natasha, went to a fortune teller six months prior, and since then, evil spirits would attack her. They believed this fortune teller had placed a spell on her. These spirits would cut her flesh and said they were going to kill her. You could not see the spirits, but you could see the damage to her body. These students were right; these were demons, but I said to the Lord, "I'm tired." He replied, "I am not." It did not feel like good news to me then, but it is good that God is never tired.

It is as Psalm 121:3–4 (NASB) says, *"He will not allow your foot to slip; He who watches over you will not slumber. Behold, He who watches over Israel will neither slumber nor sleep."* When we are tired, God is not. When we are weak, He is strong. When we look to him and lean on him, He shows up and shows off.

We found this girl, Natasha, with her grandmother, and she looked awful. Her head was down, and her arms were bleeding. We gathered round and we cast the devil out of her. Nothing big, nothing splashy. Then we led her and her grandmother to the Lord, because if you do not get Jesus in your heart, those demons will return stronger (Matthew 12:43–45). When I returned to Ukraine eight months later, Natasha — still healed, still free — greeted me at the airport. All her family was now saved. How did this happen? Not because I was strong, but because God is strong. I had grace, yes, but I also had *dunamis* power. When you feel the weakest, that is when God can bring the greatest miracle-working power.

Remember, God's grace is Him giving His supernatural ability to what we face. In my weakness, all of

Natasha's family saw God's mighty ability. In reflecting on God's grace in his thorn, Paul wrote, *"Most gladly I will rather boast in my infirmities, that the power of Christ may rest upon me"* (2 Corinthians 12:9). We all want to keep experiencing God's power, but it is as we face ongoing weakness that the power of Christ comes to rest on us and stays a while. Usually, we are rebuking the devil when he tries to take our health and provision, and we should, but we can still take pleasure in these thorns because of how God will redeem them. This is why we do not despise our thorns. God can use them to bring the greatest blessing to our lives.

MEANT FOR GOOD

These stories of God using thorns to bless His people are all over the Bible. Look at Joseph's brothers selling him into slavery. You think you have a bad job? Joseph did not even have any rights, let alone a paycheck! Still, even there, the Bible says God was with him (Genesis 39:2). Even if you are at a miserable job, the Lord is with you. You can make the best of the situation by realizing that your relationship with God and honoring Him is more important than liking your job.

Despite still honoring God, for 13 years, every time Joseph's life seemed like it might get better, things got worse. He was falsely imprisoned for a crime he did not commit. Then overnight, he went from prison to being second in command over all of Egypt. Still another 10 years went by before he was reunited with his brothers. Despite their evil towards him, Joseph was gracious to them in their time of famine, saying, *"Do not be afraid, for am I in the place of God? But as for you, you meant evil against me; but God meant it for good, in order to bring it about as it is this day, to save many people alive"* (Genesis 50:19–20). The good was not just for Joseph, but for the whole nation.

Remember, God's grace is Him giving His supernatural ability to what we face.

Paul was imprisoned more than anybody in the Bible, yet he wrote many of his epistles from jail. Generations of Christians have caught Paul's revelation of God because his thorn of imprisonment brought blessing. This good was not just for the apostle Paul, but for the whole body of Christ.

Thorns may be meant for evil against you, but God means them for good. In a battle of wills, God's will is what will be done. These stories are a reminder that the greater the suffering, the greater the anointing.

These stories are not just in the Bible though. You can find them in your local church. Where Paul saw God's beauty in the ugliness of jail, I saw God's beauty in my ugly little house in Amarillo, Texas. It was a miserable little place loaded with cockroaches and mice, but that is where I learned God called me to teach His Word. It changed the trajectory of my whole life. Looking back, I thank God for those cockroaches and mice because it made it easier to look to Him.

I knew a wonderful schoolteacher who was demoted for his faithfulness. His Bible study brought a hundred teenagers to Jesus, but one parent reported him to the principal. This schoolteacher, extensively educated and greatly successful, was unfairly demoted and looked down on. This demotion did not just impact this man, but also his wife and four teenagers. Still, this family patiently endured. They stayed in church, they stayed in the Word, and they stayed true to God. It was in church that this schoolteacher met a representative from Oral Roberts University. Overnight, he went from being demoted to becoming the head of ORU's music department. All four of his teenagers received an education from ORU that this schoolteacher would likely not have been able to afford otherwise. Three of his sons now have doctorates, and their kids are missionaries. The thorn of demotion from Satan was meant for evil, but God took it and used it for good. This good was not just for the schoolteacher but for his whole family.

The greater the suffering, the greater the anointing.

We must remember that thorns are temporary, but the blessings last. Sometimes the temporariness of thorns is long. Once, a local newspaper trashed our church on the front page. Even if you were just walking by the newsstand, you could read the hate on the cover. It hurt and it looked ugly, but we chose to be blessed by it. When I feared people would leave the church over this, none did, and others even came to check us out from the coverage. Decades later, this same newspaper wrote that my daughter and son-in-law had the best church in town. No, it was not on the front cover — that does not sell — but what was a longstanding thorn became a blessing to me.

Sometimes the temporariness of thorns is short, but the threat feels high. In 2005, I was set to take part in a massive gathering in a cricket stadium in Pakistan, but the local government warned us of 34 suicide bombers. They discovered this threat when they arrested 16 of them with written plans to blow up the stadium and would not permit us to meet. These bombing plans included my picture! This was way worse than having my picture in a bad newspaper article. My team wanted to leave; the embassy warned us to leave, but I remembered how Jesus called us to pray for our enemies (Matthew 5:43–47). So, I prayed for them. I may not know this side of heaven what happened to them, but I know I never would have prayed for my enemies without this thorn. Disciples of Jesus love their enemies. That is us! We need to love our enemies.

After we prayed, the mood lightened a bit in our team. Someone joked that if we did die, it would be a "shortcut to glory!" and this became our slogan for the trip. Instead, the Catholic church welcomed us onto their grounds for our gathering. No one saw that one coming! Looking back, I can see several times where

God used the thorn of an enemy to refine me. I should not be surprised. After all, Jesus died for His enemies:

> *God demonstrates His own love toward us, in that while we were still sinners, Christ died for us. Much more then, having now been justified by His blood, we shall be saved from wrath through Him. For if when we were enemies we were reconciled to God through the death of His Son, much more, having been reconciled, we shall be saved by His life.*
> ROMANS 5:8–10

It is a beautiful thing to be saved by the life of Christ. In him, everything is reconcilable, even an enemy.

BUFFET BONDED

In closing this chapter on how God can use thorns to bless us, I want to look at the words of Paul near the end of his life. He was once again imprisoned, and as he reflected upon all that he endured over the years and all that he chose to give up, he wrote that it was all worth it, *"that I may know Him and the power of His resurrection, and the fellowship of His sufferings"* (Philippians 3:10).

This is not the kind of bonding most people want, but it is the fellowship Jesus offers. I know what it means to lament what was lost. I know what it means to give up the good things in life to choose the great pursuits of God. I know what it means to endure thorns, but it is here that I have also seen the power of the resurrection. It is with these painful, blessed thorns that I have entered the fellowship of Jesus' sufferings. Why is it that my favorite people in church are those who have endured hard times but came out more faithful than ever? It is because we have this fellowship of suffering. We did not get bitter. We saw the power of the resurrection, and through these thorns, we came to know God more.

The thorns of life are here to buffet you anyway. Do not miss what God is doing with you during these times of suffering. Come know him more. Come see the power of His resurrection in your weakness. Come join His fellowship.

If I have to boast, I will boast of

what pertains to my weakness.

2 CORINTHIANS 11:30 NASB

"Do not be afraid, for am I in the place of God? But as for you, you meant evil against me; but God meant it for good, in order to bring it about as it is this day, to save many people alive."

GENESIS 50:19–20

CHAPTER NINE

FIVE POWERS FOR EVERY BELIEVER

*Finally, brethren, rejoice, be made complete,
be comforted, be like-minded, live in peace;
and the God of love and peace will be with you.*

2 CORINTHIANS 13:11 NASB

Everyone desires the power of God, because power gives us an opportunity to win in a situation. We have all felt powerless in life. Feeling powerless makes you feel like you cannot win, but when we read the Word, you see that God's power is used in some unique circumstances.

This power is not only for super Christians, but for every believer. Remember that God's power:

- Brings all comfort to all suffering and helps us comfort others (2 Corinthians 1:3–4).
- Lovingly corrects without crushing us (2:6–11).
- Always causes us to triumph in Christ (2:14).
- Transforms us (3:18), is excellent (4:7), and is released by speaking the Word (4:13).
- Causes thanksgiving (4:15), equips us with grace, and teaches us to patiently endure (6:6).
- Conquers the negative strongholds of our thought life (10:3–6).
- Uses thorns meant for evil to bless us. He is strong when we are weak (12:7–10).

Knowing this, here are five excellent powers for every believer:

Power Against Satan

In the previous chapter, I wrote about how although the demonic purpose of the enemy is to torment you, God's divine repurpose of these thorns is to refine you. Your pain can become gain. You can become better, not bitter.

That is how powerful God is — He takes even what is designed to be your worst and can make it your best.

I had the privilege of meeting Wong Ming Dao. He was one of the greatest Christians in China and helped grow the house church movement. When communists came in, they knew he was a gifted preacher, and they imprisoned him for his faith. They were so cruel that he denied Christ. Upon doing so, they let him out. This freedom tormented him, and he had a nervous breakdown. It was so bad that his faithful friends encouraged him to speak the truth of his faith. "Go and tell them to put you back in prison because you believe in Jesus," they said. "This time you won't give Him up. Take Jesus into your prison."

This time, the thorn of unjust imprisonment did not break Wong Ming Dao. They even arrested his wife. Now people came and said, "You need to deny Jesus," but he knew better. It was better to be imprisoned with Christ than free without Him. The guards told him he would never get out, but after 22 years, Wong Ming Dao walked free. I asked him, "How did you stand it in prison all those years?" and he replied, "I lived in the glory of God." This is the same excellent power God has given every believer, that when you face the worst the devil has to throw at you, with Jesus, you can still live in the glory of God. You can win!

Power for Ministry

Second Corinthians 6:7 says that we have the truth of the Bible, the miracle-working *dunamis* power of God, and the armor of righteousness protecting us on both sides. I have been in ministry long enough that I can tell you that ministry must have God's power. Otherwise, all human effort falls short. Without God's power for ministry, you will not see godly fellowship, you will not see the truth of the Word bring repentance, and you will not see healing, but with God, all things are possible (Matthew 19:26). Ministry is all about living in God's possible.

You can become better, not bitter.

I remember ministering to the underground church of Romania. Given the threat, everything about that trip required care, but no matter how careful you are, life happens. As four of us drove between towns to minister to the next underground church in Oradea, we ran out of gas. It was very dark out there at night, but one of our team members said he would walk to the next town for help. However, if he did that, we would miss the opportunity to minister. I asked, "Can I stand by the roadside and try to stop a car?" He replied, "Not in this country. It's too dangerous. Besides, you don't even know the language. How could you tell them?"

I understood, but I still wanted to try. Not many cars came by, but one stopped. This one car had a couple who spoke English, and huge cans of gasoline in the trunk, and they were willing to share. With the delay, we were late to the meeting, and we felt hurried, but God is not in a hurry. He always has the fuel to minister. It was another night where I did not feel spiritual enough, but when we arrived at this meeting, I saw a growth on the pastor's head, and God said, "I want to take the growth off his head in front of these people." Sure enough, I prayed, God moved, and the man's head was healed. These days, he has a big church in Oradea, and he remains healed.

God gives power for ministry. It is available in us. If you have Jesus, you have miracle-working power for ministry that works far beyond your limitations.

Power for Giving

I already mentioned in chapter five how God can move in our finances when we care about what He cares about. In 2 Corinthians 8, Paul gathered funds for the churches of Macedonia. They faced "deep poverty" (8:2), but Paul called the church of Corinth to abound in the grace of giving (8:7). Let me tell you, sowing money into what and who God cares about may not feel easy, but God extends His ability to those who choose to give.

God has miracle-working power for giving. He can cover the need in the most unusual ways. How else could the ministry God gave me reach so many? If you will make yourself available to give and to listen to where God tells you to give, He has the *dunamis* miracle-working power for the situation.

Back when I first started, it cost $60 a month to be on the radio five days a week. Sixty dollars felt like a lot then, but with prices today, I laugh. Today, my daughter, granddaughter, and I still reach many people on our programs. It has all come from supernatural giving. As we take part in supernatural giving, we also get to take part in supernatural receiving (2 Corinthians 8:14–15).

Power for Relationships

In chapter two, I wrote about how people can be your test. Relationships can be such a challenge! People may be troublesome; we may even be hard to get along with at times, but Jesus died for His enemies. He gives us the ministry of reconciliation (2 Corinthians 5:18). Remember, reconciling people to Christ is a supernatural ministry. We do not simply relate to people by our own efforts.

> Sowing money into what and who God cares about may not feel easy, but God extends his ability to those who choose to give.

For years, I had an aunt who was negative toward ministry. She had encouraged me in my education and was supportive of my desire to be an ambassador to foreign nations. But then I met my husband, got Spirit-filled, became "too radical," and all my plans fell by the wayside. My aunt could not see why I would pursue ministry over education. She said, "You could have gotten your doctorate in foreign languages, but instead you've thrown your life away!"

My aunt was dear to me, like a second mother, so those words hurt. I still wanted to honor her, and I still longed for her approval. I visited her once a year, but she did not even want to tell her friends that I was married to a pastor. Still, God gave me love and patience for my aunt. It was many years later that she began to ask questions, "Are you on the radio? My friends say you're quite good." I had never told her, because I did not want her to cast it aside, but my aunt began listening to my teaching on the radio. Then, she started coming to my meetings when I was in her town, and God healed her of a horrible knee condition. In seeing God allow me to be an ambassador for Christ to many nations, my aunt began to value ministry. Right before she died, she told me, "I'm so proud of you and what you do," but there were many years where I had to live by the supernatural power of God in that relationship. His power and grace are enough!

Power for Leadership

If we need God's power just to relate to people well, it should be no surprise that we need God's power to lead people well.

Before giving his closing greetings to the church in Corinth, Paul stated, *"I write these things being absent, lest being present I should use sharpness, according to the authority which the Lord has given me for edification and not for destruction"* (2 Corinthians 13:10). First, we know that while there is power in leadership, that power is given by God and He can remove it. Jesus does not need any of us, but He chooses to work with us for our good and His glory. For this reason, we remember that our leadership should reflect His. We are to edify people, not destroy them. For power to be good, it needs to work in the right way, not the strongest way.

THE FINAL WORD

Despite all the times of joy and suffering where I now recognize God's faithfulness, I still need to hear His voice in my life today. For all that I may still face, I return to the guidance of the Good Shepherd.

For me, there is no part of the Bible where Jesus speaks more clearly than in His farewell discourse in John 14–17. It is nearly all red letters — the spoken words of Jesus. The cross was coming, but Jesus took those final, fleeting moments to tell His closest followers what they truly needed to know.

Right before, Jesus reminded them of His love (John 13). He told them of some of the suffering they would face (15:18–16:6), and that He would turn their grief into joy (16:16–24). Jesus told them He would send the paraclete of the Holy Spirit to comfort and empower them (14:15–31; 16:7–15), and then He prayed for the disciples and all future believers (John 17).

> **We are to edify people, not destroy them. For power to be good, it needs to work in the right way, not the strongest way.**

Judas had already set out in the dark of night to betray Christ. The soldiers would soon be coming to arrest him. After three years together, these were the last words Jesus would say to His closest followers before His death. When you know someone is about to die, you really listen, and Jesus, knowing the suffering He would soon face and the suffering His disciples would later face, really knew what to say. He still speaks these words to His sheep today:

> *"I am the true vine, and my Father is the gardener. He cuts off every branch in me that bears no fruit, while every branch that does bear fruit he prunes*

so that it will be even more fruitful. You are already clean because of the word I have spoken to you. Remain in me, as I also remain in you. No branch can bear fruit by itself; it must remain in the vine. Neither can you bear fruit unless you remain in me.

"I am the vine; you are the branches. If you remain in me and I in you, you will bear much fruit; apart from me you can do nothing. If you do not remain in me, you are like a branch that is thrown away and withers; such branches are picked up, thrown into the fire and burned. If you remain in me and my words remain in you, ask whatever you wish, and it will be done for you. This is to my Father's glory, that you bear much fruit, showing yourselves to be my disciples."
JOHN 15:1–8 NIV

Do you know what the Bible describes as humanity's first home? A garden. In Genesis 2, the garden of Eden is a place of peace where people had true harmony with God before sin came into the world. Do you know what the last chapter of the Bible describes? That same garden restored and transformed.

Revelation 22:1–3 (NIV) even describes a redeemed tree of life, similar to the tree Adam and Eve ate from. John writes, *"Then the angel showed me the river of the water of life, as clear as crystal, flowing from the throne of God and of the Lamb down the middle of the great street of the city. On each side of the river stood the tree of life, bearing twelve crops of fruit, yielding its fruit every month. And the leaves of the tree are for the healing of the nations. No longer will there be any curse. The throne of God and of the Lamb will be in the city, and his servants will serve him."*

And where does Jesus go right after His farewell discourse (John 18)? Where does He cry out to His heavenly Father right before He sets all things right by the suffering and redemption of the cross? That's right: A garden. This is what Jesus prayed there:

> *He said to them, "My soul is exceedingly sorrowful, even to death. Stay here and watch." He went a little farther, and fell on the ground, and prayed that if it were possible, the hour might pass from Him. And He said, "Abba, Father, all things are possible for You. Take this cup away from Me; nevertheless, not what I will, but what You will."*
>
> MARK 14:34–36

While the garden of Gethsemane is known as the place where Jesus is betrayed and arrested, this garden was a place where He regularly met with His disciples (John 18:1–2). Your life is a garden, one that is in the hands of almighty God. I do not understand all the ways God chooses to grow and prune our lives — I do not think we are meant to — but I know that He is a good gardener. He knows better than we do. This is why we pray, even in the greatest of sufferings, that His will be done. This is why we remain in Him. The Father knows what He is doing through the true vine of Jesus. I know that outside of Him we can do nothing, but by remaining in Him we can bear fruit to God's glory. We cannot allow suffering to get in the way. We must let suffering make us better disciples. Then, our pain becomes gain.

Still today, I remain in Christ and His words remain in me, so this is what I ask: That with the time I have left, I still get to cover the earth with the Word. I think about what my last words will be, and God willing, I hope they strengthen people to live their lives from knowing the mighty and redemptive love of Jesus. It is as that old hymn says:

I come to the garden alone
While the dew is still on the roses
And the voice I hear falling on my ear
The Son of God discloses.

And He walks with me, and He talks with me
And He tells me I am His own
And the joy we share as we tarry there
None other has ever known.

Your life is a garden, one that is in the hands of almighty God.

I pray you walk with Jesus through all seasons and hear His voice. I pray you know the fullness of your adoption into His kingdom as a beloved child. And I pray that you will know the joy that only Jesus can give to you through your challenging, beautiful, and fruitful life. There is a good garden waiting.

END NOTES

A Note from Marilyn

"No pain, no gain" is attributed to Jane Fonda: *ACFAOM.org*, 2005, web.archive.org/web/20080405042036/http://www.acfaom.org/pain.shtml (accessed September 5, 2024).

Transfigured; transformed: James Strong. "Metamorphóō" in *The New Strong's Complete Dictionary of Bible Words*. (Nashville: Thomas Nelson, Inc., 1996), 262.

Chapter 1

Over 70 times . . . "Strength" in Bible Gateway: biblegateway.com/quicksearch/?qs_version=NKJV&quicksearch=strength&begin=23&end=23 (accessed September 9, 2024).

The narrow place: "thlipsis" in Bible Hub: biblehub.com/greek/2347.htm (accessed September 9, 2024).

Sufferings of Christ: James Strong. "pathema" in *The New Strong's Complete Dictionary of Bible Words*. (Nashville: Thomas Nelson, Inc., 1996), 672.

Longsuffering: James Strong. "hypomonē" in *The New Strong's Complete Dictionary of Bible Words*. (Nashville: Thomas Nelson, Inc., 1996), 719.

"Hurt people hurt people" is attributed to Charles Eads: "Polk Street Professor" in *Amarillo Globe-Times* (Amarillo, TX: February 2, 1959), page 30, column 1. quoteinvestigator.com/2019/09/15/hurt (accessed September 9. 2024).

Paraclete: James Strong. "Paráklētos" in *The New Strong's Complete Dictionary of Bible Words*. (Nashville: Thomas Nelson, Inc., 1996), 52.

The most often repeated commandment . . . "'Remember' makes frequent appearance in the Bible," in *The Jerusalem Post*, March 29, 2012: jpost.com/christian-in-israel/bible-commentary/remember-makes-frequent-appearance-in-bible (accessed September 10, 2024).

Chapter 3

Experts believe our sense of smell . . . "The Connections Between Smell, Memory, and Health" in *Harvard Medicine*: magazine.hms.harvard.edu/articles/connections-between-smell-memory-and-health (accessed September 16, 2024).

Salvation is deliverance. James Strong. "Sōtēria" in *The New Strong's Complete Dictionary of Bible Words*. (Nashville: Thomas Nelson, Inc., 1996), 709.

Chapter 4

There is a story . . . Corrie ten Boom. *The Hiding Place* (Washington Depot, Connecticut: Chosen Books, 1971): guideposts.org/positive-living/guideposts-classics-corrie-ten-boom-forgiveness (excerpt accessed September 17, 2024).

Chapter 5

Jehovah-Jireh does not simply mean . . . "What does it mean that God is Jehovah-Jireh?" in Got Questions: gotquestions.org/Jehovah-Jireh.html (accessed September 19, 2024).

Thankfulness improves . . . "The Science of Gratitude" in Mindful: mindful.org/the-science-of-gratitude (accessed September 23, 2024).

Authority power. James Strong. "Exousia" in *The New Strong's Complete Dictionary of Bible Words*. (Nashville: Thomas Nelson, Inc., 1996), 618.

Miracle-working power. James Strong. "Dunamis" in *The New Strong's Complete Dictionary of Bible Words*. (Nashville: Thomas Nelson, Inc., 1996), 606.

If a man would actually give his own son . . . Don Richardson. *Peace Child* (Ada, Michigan: Baker Publishing Group, 2005): wikipedia.org/wiki/Don_Richardson_(missionary) (quote accessed September 23, 2024).

Chapter 6

hypomonē is used for enduring . . . : James Strong. "hypomonē" in *The New Strong's Complete Dictionary of Bible Words*. (Nashville: Thomas Nelson, Inc., 1996), 719.

830,000 members. "O come all ye faithful" in *The Economist*. November 3, 2007: economist.com/special-report/2007/11/03/o-come-all-ye-faithful (accessed November 11, 2024).

There are now more people who identify as Christian than Buddhist. "Korea, South" in the World Fact Book: cia.gov/the-world-factbook/countries/korea-south/#people-and-society (accessed November 14, 2024).

Chapter 8

Some say his thorn was . . . "What was Paul's thorn in the flesh?" in Got Questions?: gotquestions.org/Paul-thorn-flesh.html (accessed October 3, 2024).

To buffet someone means . . . "Buffet" in Merriam Webster: merriam-webster.com/dictionary/buffet (accessed October 7, 2024).

Despite still honoring God, for 13 years . . . "Joseph" in The Biblical Timeline: thebiblicaltimeline.org/joseph (accessed October 3, 2024).

I come to the garden alone . . . "In the Garden (1912 Song)" in Wikipedia: wikipedia.org/wiki/In_the_Garden_(1912_song) (accessed October 2, 2024).

RECEIVE JESUS CHRIST AS LORD AND SAVIOR OF YOUR LIFE

If you confess with your mouth the Lord Jesus and believe in your heart that God has raised Him from the dead, you will be saved. For with the heart one believes unto righteousness, and with the mouth confession is made unto salvation.

ROMANS 10:9–10

Would you like to begin a personal relationship with God and Jesus right now? You can! Simply pray this prayer in sincerity:

Heavenly Father, I acknowledge that I need your help. I am not able to change my life or circumstances through my own efforts. I know that I have made some wrong decisions in my life, and at this moment, I turn away from those ways of thinking and acting. I believe you have provided a way for me through Jesus to receive your blessings and help in my life. Right now, I believe and confess Jesus as my Lord and Savior. I ask Jesus to come into my heart and give me a new life, by your Spirit. I thank you for saving me, and I ask for your grace and mercy in my life. I pray this in Jesus' name. Amen.

If you just prayed to make Jesus your Lord, we want to know!

Please call us today at 888-637-4545.

We will pray for you and send you a special gift to help you in your new life with Christ.

ABOUT MARILYN

As founder and president of *Marilyn & Sarah Ministries*, a non-profit ministry and humanitarian organization based in Denver, Colorado, Marilyn has traveled to over 140 countries and has impacted many nations around the world — from disaster relief efforts in Haiti, Indonesia, and Pakistan to providing food for the hungry in Mexico, Costa Rica, Russia, and the Philippines.

Her legacy includes significant ministry in Islamic countries. In 2016, over one million people attended her healing meeting in Karachi, Pakistan.

Marilyn has held audiences with government leaders and heads of state all over the world. She was the first woman to join the board of directors for Dr. David Yonggi Cho (founder of the world's largest congregation, Yoido Full Gospel Church in South Korea).

Along with her daughter, Pastor Sarah Bowling, she co-hosts the daily television program, *Today with Marilyn & Sarah*, which is broadcast globally in nearly 200 countries with a potential viewing audience of over 2 billion households worldwide. Marilyn has also authored over 100 publications.

She and her late husband, Wallace, were married over 50 years and have two children and five grandchildren. Marilyn holds a Bachelor of Arts in Collective Foreign Languages from the University of Northern Colorado and an Honorary Doctor of Divinity from Oral Roberts University.

In 2015, Marilyn was honored at Oral Roberts University with the prestigious Lifetime Global Achievement Award. This award recognizes individuals, or organizations, that have made a significant impact in the history of ORU and around the world. In 2019, Marilyn also received an International Lifetime Peace Award from the Grand Imam and President of Pakistan.

In 2021, Marilyn was honored with two awards from the Assemblies of God Theological Seminary: The Pillar of Faith Award in acknowledgment of her worldwide impact on the church through biblical teaching and sustainable healing ministry; and the Smith Wigglesworth Award, given on behalf of the entire Assemblies of God fellowship in acknowledgment of her decades of service worldwide.

Marilyn's greatest passion and desire is to continue being a bridge-builder in countries around the world.

LEARN MORE ABOUT MARILYN & SARAH MINISTRIES

Marilyn & Sarah Ministries: marilynandsarah.org
Check out our free downloads that include Bible reading plans, teaching notes, inspirational graphics, spiritual self-assessments, and lists of verses based on topic.

Online Master Classes: mentoredbymarilyn.org
Marilyn is passing her mantle on to you! Through her anointed master classes, you will be mentored in strategic areas that will take you to the next level of victory and fulfillment in your life and ministry. This is an incredible opportunity to be mentored by Marilyn!

Connect with Marilyn:

- MarilynHickeyMinistries
- MarilynandSarah
- MarilynHickeyMinistries
- MarilynHickeyMinistries